Contents

Bake 15 to 20 minutes more, until firm. Let cool completely in baking dish. Sprinkle with confectioners' sugar and cut into 12 triangles.

In a large bowl, combine milk, chocolate pudding mix, and vanilla pudding mix. Beat until thick. Pour over cream cheese layer. Top with remaining whipped topping, and sprinkle with crushed chocolate bars.

FRUIT PIZZA

Servings: 8 | Prep: 30m | Cooks: 0m | Total: 30m

NUTRITION FACTS

Calories: 535 | Carbohydrates: 62.9g | Fat: 30g | Protein: 5.5g | Cholesterol: 49mg

INGREDIENTS

- 1 (18 ounce) package refrigerated sugar cookie dough
- 1 tablespoon cornstarch
- 1 (8 ounce) package cream cheese, softened
- 1/2 cup orange juice
- 1 (8 ounce) container frozen whipped topping, thawed
- 2 tablespoons lemon juice
- 2 cups sliced fresh strawberries
- 1/4 cup water
- 1/2 cup white sugar
- 1/2 teaspoon orange zest

1 pinch salt

DIRECTIONS

1. Preheat oven to 350 degrees F (175 degrees C). Slice cookie dough and arrange on greased pizza pan, overlapping edges. Press dough flat into pan. Bake for 10 to 12 minutes. Allow to cool.
2. In a large bowl, soften cream cheese, then fold in the whipped topping. Spread over cooled crust. You can chill for a while at this point, or continue by arranging the fruit.
3. Begin with strawberries, sliced in half. Arrange in a circle around the outside edge. Continue with fruit of your choice, working towards the middle. If bananas are used, dip them in lemon juice so they don't darken. Then make a sauce to spoon over fruit.
4. In a saucepan, combine sugar, salt, corn starch, orange juice, lemon juice and water. Cook and stir over medium heat. Bring to a boil, and cook for 1 or 2 minutes, until thickened. Remove from heat, and add grated orange rind. Allow to cool, but not set up. Spoon over fruit. Chill for two hours, then cut into wedges and serve.

CINDY'S PUMPKIN PIE

Servings: 16 | Prep: 15m | Cooks: 45m | Total: 1h

NUTRITION FACTS

Calories: 223 | Carbohydrates: 27.9g | Fat: 11.2g | Protein: 3.7g | Cholesterol: 46mg

INGREDIENTS

- 1 1/2 pints vanilla ice cream, softened
- 1 teaspoon ground cinnamon
- 3 eggs
- 1/4 teaspoon ground ginger
- 1 3/4 cups pumpkin puree
- 1/4 teaspoon ground nutmeg
- 3/4 cup white sugar
- 2 (9 inch) unbaked pie shells

1/2 teaspoon salt

DIRECTIONS

1. Preheat oven to 425 degrees F (220 degrees C.) Place ice cream near the warm oven to soften.
2. In a large bowl, whisk together the eggs. Stir in the pumpkin puree, sugar, salt, cinnamon, ginger, and nutmeg. Mix in soft ice cream until smooth. Pour filling into two 9 inch pie shells.
3. Bake for 15 minutes in the preheated oven. Reduce temperature to 350 degrees F (175 degrees C), and bake an additional 30 to 40 minutes, or until filling is set.

THREE BERRY PIE

Servings: 8 | Prep: 45m | Cooks: 45m | Total: 3h | Additional: 1h30m

NUTRITION FACTS

Calories: 361 | Carbohydrates: 48g | Fat: 17.7g | Protein: 3.8g | Cholesterol: 0mg

INGREDIENTS

- 2 cups all-purpose flour
- 1 cup fresh strawberries, halved
- 1/2 teaspoon salt
- 2 cups fresh raspberries
- 2/3 cup shortening, chilled
- 1 1/2 cups fresh blueberries
- 6 tablespoons cold water
- 1/2 cup white sugar

3 tablespoons cornstarch

DIRECTIONS

1. Combine the flour and salt. Using a pastry blender, cut in the shortening until the pieces are the size of small peas. Sprinkle 1 tablespoon of the water over part of the mixture, then gently toss with a fork. Push moistened portion to the side of the bowl. Repeat, using 1 tablespoon of water at a time,

until all is moistened. Divide the dough in half. Form each half into a ball and flatten slightly. Wrap in plastic and refrigerate for at least 30 minutes.

2. Transfer one piece of dough to a lightly floured surface. Roll the dough from the center to the edges to form a 12-inch circle. Wrap the crust around the rolling pin. Unroll it onto a 9-inch pie plate. Ease the crust into the pie plate, being careful not to stretch it. Trim the bottom crust evenly with the rim of the pie plate, and return the pastry-lined pie plate to the refrigerator.

3. In a large mixing bowl, stir together the sugar and cornstarch. Add the strawberries, raspberries, and blueberries; gently toss until berries are coated. Allow fruit mixture to stand for about 15 minutes.

4. Preheat the oven to 375 degrees F (190 degrees C). Place a baking sheet in the oven to preheat.

5. Roll out the remaining pastry for the top crust. Stir the berry mixture and pour the filling into the pastry-lined pie plate. Place the top crust over the pie and trim the edges, leaving a 1/2-inch overhang. Fold the top crust under the bottom crust, pressing lightly to seal. Crimp the edges of the crust and cut vents in the top to allow steam to escape. To prevent over-browning, cover the edge of the pie with foil.

6. Bake in the preheated oven on the baking tray for 25 minutes. Remove the foil.

7. Bake for an additional 20 to 30 minutes, or until the filling is bubbling and the crust is golden. Cool on a wire rack.

GRANDMA'S IRON SKILLET APPLE PIE
Servings: 8 | Prep: 15m | Cooks: 45m | Total: 1h15m | Additional: 15m

NUTRITION FACTS

Calories: 734 | Carbohydrates: 107.8g | Fat: 33.7g | Protein: 3.4g | Cholesterol: 49mg

INGREDIENTS

- 1/2 cup butter
- 1 cup white sugar, divided
- 1 cup brown sugar
- 2 teaspoons ground cinnamon, divided
- 5 Granny Smith apples -- peeled, cored, quartered, and thinly sliced
- 1/4 cup white sugar
- 3 (9 inch) refrigerated prerolled pie crusts

1 tablespoon butter, cut into small chunks **DIRECTIONS**

1. Preheat oven to 350 degrees F (175 degrees C).
2. Place 1/2 cup butter into a heavy cast iron skillet, and melt butter in the oven. Remove skillet and sprinkle with brown sugar; return to oven to heat while you prepare the apples.
3. Remove skillet, and place 1 refrigerated pie crust on top of the brown sugar. Top the pie crust with half the sliced apples. Sprinkle apples with 1/2 cup of sugar and 1 teaspoon of cinnamon; place a second pie crust over the apples; top the second crust with the remaining apples, and sprinkle with

1/2 cup sugar and 1 teaspoon cinnamon. Top with the third crust; sprinkle the top crust with 1/4 cup sugar, and dot with 1 tablespoon of butter. Cut 4 slits into the top crust for steam.

4. Bake in the preheated oven until the apples are tender and the crust is golden brown, about 45 minutes. Serve warm.

FRESH PEAR PIE

Servings: 8 | Prep: 40m | Cooks: 50m | Total: 5h30m | Additional: 4h

NUTRITION FACTS

Calories: 360 | Carbohydrates: 51.6g | Fat: 16.5g | Protein: 3.5g | Cholesterol: 4mg

INGREDIENTS

- 1 recipe pastry for a 9 inch double crust pie
- 1 teaspoon lemon zest
- 1/2 cup white sugar
- 5 cups peeled and sliced pears
- 3 tablespoons all-purpose flour
- 1 tablespoon butter
- ¼ teaspoon salt
- 1 tablespoon lemon juice

1 teaspoon ground cinnamon

DIRECTIONS

1. Preheat oven to 450 degrees F (230 degrees C). Place a baking sheet on the bottom oven rack.
2. Combine sugar, flour, salt, cinnamon, and lemon zest in mixing bowl. Roll out half the pastry and line a 9-inch pie pan.
3. Arrange pear slices in layers in the pastry-lined pan, sprinkling the sugar mixture over each layer. Dot with butter and sprinkle with lemon juice.
4. Roll out remaining dough for the top crust. Use your finger dipped in a small bowl of water to moisten the rim of the bottom crust. Place top crust over filling, and trim edge using kitchen shears or a sharp paring knife. Fold edge under bottom crust, pressing to seal. Flute edge. Cut slits in top crust to allow steam to escape.
5. Bake in the preheated oven on the baking sheet for 10 minutes. Reduce oven temperature to 350 degrees F (175 degrees C), and bake until crust is golden brown and filling is bubbly, 35 to 40 minutes longer. Allow to cool several hours before serving.

COCONUT CREAM PIE

Servings: 8 | Prep: 25m | Cooks: 30m | Total: 4h55m | Additional: 4h

NUTRITION FACTS

Calories: 399 | Carbohydrates: 51.1g | Fat: 18.8g | Protein: 6.9g | Cholesterol: 121mg

INGREDIENTS

- 1 cup white sugar
- 3 tablespoons butter
- 1/2 cup all-purpose flour
- 1 1/2 teaspoons vanilla extract
- 1/4 teaspoon salt
- 1 cup flaked coconut
- 3 cups milk
- 1 (9 inch) pie shell, baked

4 egg yolks

DIRECTIONS

1. In a medium saucepan, combine sugar, flour and salt over a medium heat; gradually stir in milk. Cook and stir over medium heat until the mixture is thick and bubbly. Reduce heat to low and cook 2 minutes more. Remove the pan from heat.
2. Place a strainer over a clean mixing bowl; set aside.
3. Beat the egg yolks slightly. Gradually pour 1 cup of the hot custard mixture into yolks, whisking constantly. Return the egg mixture to the saucepan and bring the entire mixture to a gentle boil. Cook and stir 2 minutes before removing the pan from heat. Immediately pour custard through the strainer.
4. Stir butter, vanilla, and coconut into the hot mixture. Pour the hot filling into the baked pie crust. Cool and refrigerate until set, about 4 hours.

EASY HOMEMADE PIE CRUST
Servings: 8 | Prep: 10m | Cooks: 30m | Total: 40m

NUTRITION FACTS

Calories: 346 | Carbohydrates: 29.8g | Fat: 23.4g | Protein: 4.3g | Cholesterol: 61mg

INGREDIENTS

- 2 1/2 cups all-purpose flour
- 7 tablespoons ice water
- 1 cup unsalted butter - chilled, cut into tablespoon-size pieces
- 1 tablespoon cider vinegar

1/2 teaspoon salt

DIRECTIONS

1. Combine flour, salt, and butter in a food processor. Pulse until mixture resembles coarse crumbs, about 10 1-second pulses.
2. Stir water and vinegar in a small bowl.
3. Pour half the ice water and vinegar mixture into the flour and butter mixture. Pulse to combine, about 3 (1-second) pulses. Pour in remaining ice water and vinegar mixture. Pulse until mixture just starts to come together, about 8 (1-second) pulses.
4. Turn dough out onto a wooden surface, pat into round shape and divide in half. Form each half into a disc about 5 inches wide.
5. Wrap each disc in plastic wrap and refrigerate for at least 30 minutes until ready to use.

CHERRY PIE

Servings: 8 | Prep: 30m | Cooks: 45m | Total: 3h | Additional: 1h45m

NUTRITION FACTS

Calories: 506 | Carbohydrates: 62.9g | Fat: 27.5g | Protein: 3.6g | Cholesterol: 4mg

INGREDIENTS

- 2 cups all-purpose flour
- 1 1/4 cups white sugar
- 1 cup shortening, chilled
- 10 teaspoons cornstarch
- 1/2 cup cold water
- 1 tablespoon butter
- 1 pinch salt
- 1/4 teaspoon almond extract

2 cups pitted sour cherries

DIRECTIONS

1. Cut the shortening into the flour and salt with the whisking blades of a stand mixer until the crumbs are pea-sized. Mix in cold water by hand just until the dough holds together. Divide the dough in half and form it into two disks. Wrap in plastic and refrigerate until chilled through, 30 minutes to 1 hour.
2. Roll out one disk of dough into a 11-inch circle. Line a 9-inch pie pan with pastry. Refrigerate until needed. Roll out the dough for the top crust, transfer it to a plate or baking sheet, and refrigerate.
3. Preheat the oven to 375 degrees F (190 degrees C). Place a baking tray in the oven to preheat.
4. Place the cherries, sugar, and cornstarch in a medium-sized non-aluminum saucepan. Allow the mixture to stand for 10 minutes, or until the sugar draws out the cherries' juices. Bring to a boil over medium heat, stirring constantly. Lower the heat; simmer for 1 minute, or until the juices thicken and become translucent. Remove pan from heat, and stir in butter and almond extract. Allow the

filling to cool to lukewarm. Pour the filling into the pie shell. Cover with top crust, crimp the edges to seal, and cut vents for steam.

5. Bake in a preheated 375 degree F (190 degree C) oven on the baking tray for 45 to 55 minutes, or until the crust is golden brown. Allow to cool for several hours before slicing.

CARAMEL APPLE PIE

Servings: 8 | Prep: 30m | Cooks: 1h | Total: 1h40m

NUTRITION FACTS

Calories: 336 | Carbohydrates: 48.2g | Fat: 16.3g | Protein: 1.7g | Cholesterol: 23mg

INGREDIENTS

- 6 tablespoons unsalted butter
- 1/4 teaspoon cinnamon
- 1/2 cup white sugar
- 1 pinch salt
- 1/2 cup brown sugar
- 5 apples - peeled, cored and sliced
- 1/4 cup water

1 pastry for double-crust pie (see footnote for recipe link)**DIRECTIONS**

1. Preheat oven to 425 degrees F (220 degrees C).
2. Combine butter, white sugar, brown sugar, water, cinnamon, and salt in a saucepan over medium heat. Bring to a boil, remove from heat and set aside.
3. Roll out half the pastry to fit a 9-inch pie plate. Place bottom crust in pie plate; pour in apple slices.
4. Roll out top crust into a 10-inch circle. Cut into 8 (1-inch) wide strips with a sharp paring knife or pastry wheel. Weave the pastry strips, one at a time, into a lattice pattern. Fold the ends of the lattice strips under the edge of the bottom crust and crimp to seal.
5. Pour butter-sugar mixture over top of pie, coating the lattice, and allowing any remaining sauce to drizzle through the crust.
6. Bake in the preheated oven for 15 minutes. Reduce heat to 350 degrees F (175 degrees C), and bake until the crust is golden brown, the caramel on the top crust is set, and the apple filling is bubbling, 35 to 40 more minutes. Allow to cool completely before slicing.

SWEET POTATO PIE

Servings: 8 | Prep: 20m | Cooks: 40m | Total: 1h

NUTRITION FACTS

Calories: 449 | Carbohydrates: 60.2g | Fat: 21.6g | Protein: 5.5g | Cholesterol: 82mg

INGREDIENTS

- 2 cups mashed sweet potatoes
- 1/2 teaspoon ground cinnamon
- 1/4 pound butter, softened
- 1/2 teaspoon ground nutmeg
- 2 eggs, separated
- 1/2 cup evaporated milk
- 1 cup packed brown sugar
- 1/4 cup white sugar
- 1/4 teaspoon salt
- 1 (9 inch) unbaked pie crust

1/2 teaspoon ground ginger

DIRECTIONS

1. Preheat oven to 400 degrees F (200 degrees C).
2. In a mixing bowl, combine the sweet potatoes, butter, egg yolks, brown sugar, salt, ginger, cinnamon, nutmeg and evaporated milk. Mix together well.
3. Beat egg whites until stiff peaks form; add 1/4 cup sugar and fold into sweet potato mixture.
4. Pour into pie shell and bake at 400 degrees F (200 degrees C) for 10 minutes. Reduce heat and bake at 350 degrees F (175 degrees C) for 30 minutes or until firm.

BLUEBERRY CRUMB PIE

Servings: 8 | Prep: 30m | Cooks: 40m | Total: 1h10m

NUTRITION FACTS

Calories: 461 | Carbohydrates: 75.6g | Fat: 17g | Protein: 4.5g | Cholesterol: 23mg

INGREDIENTS

- 1 (9 inch) unbaked pie crust
- 2/3 cup packed brown sugar
- 3/4 cup white sugar
- 3/4 cup rolled oats
- 1/3 cup all-purpose flour
- 1/2 cup all-purpose flour
- 2 teaspoons grated lemon zest
- 1/2 teaspoon ground cinnamon
- 1 tablespoon lemon juice
- 6 tablespoons butter

5 cups fresh or frozen blueberries

DIRECTIONS

1. Preheat the oven to 375 degrees F (190 degrees C).
2. Press the pie crust into the bottom and up the sides of a 9 inch pie plate. In a large bowl, stir together the sugar and flour. Mix in the lemon zest and lemon juice. Gently stir in the blueberries. Pour into the pie crust.
3. In a medium bowl, stir together the brown sugar, oats, flour and cinnamon. Mix in butter using a fork until crumbly. Spread the crumb topping evenly over the pie filling.
4. Bake for 40 minutes in the preheated oven, or until browned on top. Cool over a wire rack.

SOUR CREAM APPLE PIE DELUXE
Servings: 8 | Prep: 20m | Cooks: 1h | Total: 1h20m

NUTRITION FACTS

Calories: 382 | Carbohydrates: 48.1g | Fat: 20g | Protein: 4g | Cholesterol: 51mg

INGREDIENTS

- 1 unbaked 9 inch pie crust
- 1 egg
- 3/4 cup sugar
- 2 cups diced apples
- 2 tablespoons all-purpose flour
- 1/3 cup sugar
- 1/8 teaspoon salt
- 1/3 cup all-purpose flour
- 1 cup sour cream
- 1 teaspoon ground cinnamon
- 1/2 teaspoon vanilla extract

1/4 cup chilled butter, diced **DIRECTIONS**

1. Preheat the oven to 425 degrees F (220 degrees C). Press the pie crust into and up the sides of a 9 inch pie plate.
2. In a medium bowl, stir together 3/4 cup sugar, 2 tablespoons of flour, and salt. Mix in the sour cream, egg and vanilla until smooth. Add apples, and stir to coat. Scrape the mixture into the pie shell.
3. Bake for 15 minutes in the preheated oven, then reduce heat to 350 degrees F (175 degrees C), and continue baking for 30 minutes more.
4. While the pie is baking, prepare the topping in a medium bowl. Stir together 1/3 cup of flour, 1/3 cup sugar, and cinnamon. Cut in the butter until the mixture resembles fine crumbs.

5. After the 30 minute bake time has passed, cover the top of the pie with the crumb topping, and continue to bake for 15 minutes, or until topping is lightly browned and apples are tender. Allow the pie to cool, then refrigerate until chilled before serving.

THE OLD BOY'S STRAWBERRY PIE
Servings: 8 | Prep: 15m | Cooks: 1h | Total: 1h15m

NUTRITION FACTS

Calories: 410 | Carbohydrates: 62.9g | Fat: 16.6g | Protein: 4g | Cholesterol: 23mg**INGREDIENTS**

- 1 recipe pastry for a 9 inch single crust pie
- 4 cups fresh strawberries, hulled
- 3/4 cup white sugar
- 1/2 cup white sugar
- 3/4 cup all-purpose flour
- 1/2 cup all-purpose flour
- 6 tablespoons butter
- 1 tablespoon cornstarch

1 pinch ground nutmeg

DIRECTIONS

1. Preheat oven to 400 degrees F (200 degrees C). Place a drip pan on lowest shelf to catch pie juices.
2. To Make Topping: In a medium bowl, mix until fluffy the 3/4 cup sugar, 3/4 cup flour, butter, and nutmeg.
3. Place cleaned strawberries in a deep bowl. In a separate bowl, mix together the 1/2 cup sugar, 1/2 cup flour, and cornstarch. Gently coat berries with this mixture; be careful not to crush berries.
4. Pour berries into prepared pie crust mounding them in the middle; mounding is necessary as the berries will sink as they bake. Cover berries with crumb topping and top crumbs with about 15 pea-sized blobs of butter. Wrap edges of pie crust with foil to prevent burning.
5. Bake pie in preheated oven for 20 minutes, then reduce heat to 375 degrees F (190 degrees C) and bake for an additional 40 minutes. When there are 10 minutes left of baking, sprinkle a little extra sugar over crumb topping and then finish baking.

COCONUT CREAM PIE
Servings: 8 | Prep: 15m | Cooks: 1h15m | Total: 1hm**NUTRITION FACTS**

Calories: 358 | Carbohydrates: 42.7g | Fat: 19.8g | Protein: 3.7g | Cholesterol: 4mg

INGREDIENTS

- 1 (9 inch) pie shell, baked
- 1 1/2 cups flaked coconut
- 1 (5 ounce) package instant vanilla pudding mix
- 1 (8 ounce) container frozen whipped topping, thawed

1 1/2 cups milk**DIRECTIONS**

1. In a large bowl, combine the pudding mix and milk until the pudding mixture thickens. Fold 1 cup of coconut and half of the nondairy whipped topping into the pudding. Pour the combination into the prepared pie crust.
2. Spread the remainder of the nondairy whipped topping on top of the pie. Sprinkle with the remainder of the coconut. Refrigerate, and serve chilled.

HOMEMADE BANANA PUDDING PIE
Servings: 8 | Prep: 30m | Cooks: 30m | Total: 2h | Additional: 1h

NUTRITION FACTS

Calories: 504 | Carbohydrates: 92.1g | Fat: 12.8g | Protein: 7.2g | Cholesterol: 84mg

INGREDIENTS

- 2 cups vanilla wafer crumbs
- 3 egg yolks
- 3 bananas, sliced into 1/4 inch slices
- 2 teaspoons butter
- 1 1/2 cups white sugar
- 2 teaspoons vanilla extract
- 1/4 cup all-purpose flour
- 3 egg whites
- 2 cups milk

1/4 cup white sugar **DIRECTIONS**

1. Preheat oven to 350 degrees F (175 degrees C).
2. Line the bottom and sides of a 9-inch pie plate with a layer of alternating vanilla wafer crumbs and banana slices.
3. To Make Pudding: In a medium saucepan, combine 1 1/2 cups sugar with flour. Mix well, then stir in half the milk. Beat egg yolks and whisk into sugar mixture. Add remaining milk and butter or margarine.
4. Place mixture over low heat and cook until thickened, stirring frequently. Remove from heat and stir in vanilla extract. Pour half of pudding over vanilla wafer and banana layer while still hot.
5. Make another layer of alternating vanilla wafers and banana slices on top of pudding layer. Pour remaining pudding over second wafer and banana layer.

6. To Make Meringue: In a large glass or metal bowl, beat egg whites until foamy. Gradually add 1/4 cup sugar, continuing to beat until whites are stiff. Spread meringue into pie pan, making sure to completely cover pudding layer.
7. Bake in preheated oven for 15 minutes, just until meringue is browned. Chill before serving.

DEATH BY CHOCOLATE MOUSSE

Servings: 8 | Prep: 25m | Cooks: 5m | Total: 7h | Additional: 6h30m

NUTRITION FACTS

Calories: 835 | Carbohydrates: 61.2g | Fat: 67.4g | Protein: 5.7g | Cholesterol: 178mg

INGREDIENTS

- 21 chocolate sandwich cookies, crushed
- 1 pinch salt
- 1/4 cup butter, softened
- 2 cups heavy cream
- 1 cup heavy cream
- 1/4 cup white sugar
- 1 (12 ounce) package semisweet chocolate chips
- 1 cup heavy cream, chilled
- 1 teaspoon vanilla extract

1/4 cup white sugar **DIRECTIONS**

1. Preheat oven to 350 degrees F (175 degrees C). Generously grease a 9 inch springform pan with 2 3/4 inch sides.
2. In a medium bowl, mix together crushed cookies and softened butter or margarine. Press mixture evenly into greased pan. Bake in preheated oven for 5 minutes, then allow to cool.
3. Combine 1 cup cream, chocolate, vanilla extract, and salt, in the top of a double boiler. Heat until chocolate is fully melted and mixture is smooth. Alternatively, if you have a food processor, you can blend mixture by placing chocolate, vanilla extract, and salt, in processor bowl. Bring 1 cup cream to a boil on stovetop, then slowly pour cream into processor with blade running. Continue to process until mixture is smooth.
4. Pour chocolate mixture into a bowl and cool to room temperature, stirring occasionally.
5. In a large bowl, beat 2 cups chilled cream with 1/4 cup sugar. Beat until stiff peaks form. Fold whipped cream into chocolate mixture. Pour mixture into cooled crust.
6. Chill pie at least 6 hours before serving. Prior to serving, beat remaining 1 cup cream with 1/4 cup sugar. Beat until stiff, then pipe onto top of pie with a star tip, or place a spoonful on top of each slice.

PEANUT BUTTER PIE

Servings: 8 | Prep: 30m | Cooks: 10m | Total: 4h40m | Additional: 4h

NUTRITION FACTS

Calories: 652 | Carbohydrates: 51.9g | Fat: g | Protein: 12g | Cholesterol: 91mg

INGREDIENTS

- 1 1/4 cups chocolate cookie crumbs
- 1 cup white sugar
- 1/4 cup white sugar
- 1 tablespoon unsalted butter, softened
- 1/4 cup butter
- 1 teaspoon vanilla extract
- 1 (8 ounce) package cream cheese, softened
- 1 cup heavy whipping cream

1 cup creamy peanut butter

DIRECTIONS

1. Preheat oven to 375 degrees F (190 degrees C).
2. Combine 1 1/4 cup cookie crumbs, 1/4 cup sugar, and 1/4 cup butter; press into a 9-inch pie plate. Bake in preheated oven for 10 minutes. Cool on wire rack.
3. In a mixing bowl, beat cream cheese, peanut butter, 1 cup sugar, 1 tablespoon butter, and vanilla until smooth. Whip the cream, and fold into the peanut butter mixture.
4. Gently spoon filing into crust. Garnish pie with chocolate or cookie crumbs if desired. Refrigerate for several hours before serving.

BAKED FRESH CHERRY PIE

Servings: 8 | Prep: 30m | Cooks: 50m | Total: 3h20m | Additional: 2h

NUTRITION FACTS

Calories: 410 | Carbohydrates: 60.9g | Fat: 17.8g | Protein: 3.7g | Cholesterol: 6mg

INGREDIENTS

- 1 recipe pastry for a 9 inch double crust pie
- 4 cups pitted cherries
- 4 tablespoons quick-cooking tapioca
- 1/4 teaspoon almond extract
- 1/8 teaspoon salt

- 1/2 teaspoon vanilla extract
- 1 cup white sugar

1 1/2 tablespoons butter **DIRECTIONS**

1. Preheat oven to 400 degrees F (205 degrees C). Place bottom crust in pie pan. Set top crust aside, covered.
2. In a large mixing bowl combine tapioca, salt, sugar, cherries, and extracts. Let stand 15 minutes. Turn out into bottom crust and dot with butter. Cover with top crust, flute edges and cut vents in top. Place pie on a foil-lined cookie sheet--in case of drips!
3. Bake for 50 minutes in the preheated oven, until golden brown. Let cool for several hours before slicing.

FRESH STRAWBERRY PIE
Servings: 16 | Prep: 15m | Cooks: 15m | Total: 2h30m | Additional: 2h

NUTRITION FACTS

Calories: 167 | Carbohydrates: 31.6g | Fat: 4.4g | Protein: 1.7g | Cholesterol: 0mg

INGREDIENTS

- 2 (8 inch) pie shells, baked
- 2 tablespoons cornstarch
- 2 1/2 quarts fresh strawberries
- 1 cup boiling water
- 1 cup white sugar

1 (3 ounce) package strawberry flavored Jell-O**DIRECTIONS**

1. In a saucepan, mix together the sugar and corn starch; make sure to blend corn starch in completely. Add boiling water, and cook over medium heat until mixture thickens. Remove from heat. Add gelatin mix, and stir until smooth. Let mixture cool to room temperature.
2. Place strawberries in baked pie shells; position berries with points facing up. Pour cooled gel mixture over strawberries.
3. Refrigerate until set. Serve with whipped cream, if desired.

MOM'S PUMPKIN PIE
Servings: 8 | Prep: 30m | Cooks: 1h | Total: 1h30m

NUTRITION FACTS

Calories: 345 | Carbohydrates: 44.3g | Fat: 16.5g | Protein: 6.6g | Cholesterol: 119mg

INGREDIENTS

- 1 recipe pastry for a 9 inch single crust pie
- 1/2 teaspoon ground nutmeg
- 3 eggs
- 1/2 teaspoon ground ginger
- 1 egg yolk
- 1/4 teaspoon ground cloves
- 1/2 cup white sugar
- 1 1/2 cups milk
- 1/2 cup packed brown sugar
- 1/2 cup heavy whipping cream
- 1 teaspoon salt
- 2 cups pumpkin puree

1/2 teaspoon ground cinnamon

DIRECTIONS

1. Preheat oven to 425 degrees F (220 degrees C.)
2. In a large bowl, combine eggs, egg yolk, white sugar and brown sugar. Add salt, cinnamon, nutmeg, ginger and cloves. Gradually stir in milk and cream. Stir in pumpkin. Pour filling into pie shell.
3. Bake for ten minutes in preheated oven. Reduce heat to 350 degrees F (175 degrees C), and bake for an additional 40 to 45 minutes, or until filling is set.

FUDGY CHOCOLATE CREAM PIE

Servings: 8 | Prep: 20m | Cooks: 25m | Total: 4h45m | Additional: 4h

NUTRITION FACTS

Calories: 315 | Carbohydrates: 47g | Fat: 13.4g | Protein: 4.6g | Cholesterol: 110mg

INGREDIENTS

- 1 (9 inch) pie crust, baked
- 4 egg yolks
- 1 1/4 cups white sugar
- 2 (1 ounce) squares unsweetened chocolate, chopped
- 2 tablespoons all-purpose flour
- 1 tablespoon butter
- 2 tablespoons cornstarch
- 1 teaspoon vanilla extract

1/4 teaspoon salt**DIRECTIONS**

1. In medium saucepan, combine sugar, flour, cornstarch and salt and whisk to combine. In a medium bowl, whisk milk and egg yolks until smooth. Gradually stir into sugar mixture. Cook over medium heat, stirring constantly, until mixture thickens and comes to a full boil. Boil and stir for one minute.
2. Remove from heat and stir in chocolate, butter, and vanilla. Stir until melted.
3. Pour into pie shell. Place plastic wrap over filling to prevent skin from forming and chill for several hours. Top with meringue or whipped cream and chocolate curls if so desired.

PECAN PIE
Servings: 8 | Prep: 20m | Cooks: 55m | Total: 1h15m

NUTRITION FACTS

Calories: 530 | Carbohydrates: 72.9g | Fat: 26.5g | Protein: 5.3g | Cholesterol: 77mg

INGREDIENTS

- 3 eggs
- 2 tablespoons butter
- 1 cup brown sugar
- 1 teaspoon vanilla extract
- 1 tablespoon all-purpose flour
- 1 1/2 cups pecans
- 1 cup corn syrup

1 (9 inch) unbaked pie shell **DIRECTIONS**

1. Preheat oven to 350 degrees F (175 degrees C). Place pie shell in a 9 inch pie pan.
2. In a medium bowl, gently beat eggs. Stir in sugar and flour, then the syrup, butter and vanilla. Fold in pecans. Pour mixture into pie shell. Bake for 50 to 60 minutes; knife inserted in center of pie should come out clean.

EASY APPLE PIE
Servings: 8 | Prep: 30m | Cooks: 50m | Total: 2h20m

NUTRITION FACTS

Calories: 454 | Carbohydrates: 56.6g | Fat: 25g | Protein: 3.4g | Cholesterol: 23mg

INGREDIENTS

- 6 tablespoons unsalted butter
- 1/4 teaspoon ground cinnamon
- 1/4 cup white sugar
- 1/4 cup water

- 1/2 cup brown sugar
- 1 (15 ounce) package double crust ready-to-use pie crust (such as Pillsbury)
- 1 pinch salt

4 large red apples, cored and thinly sliced**DIRECTIONS**

1. Preheat oven to 425 degrees F (220 degrees C).
2. Melt butter in saucepan over medium heat. Stir in white sugar, brown sugar, salt, cinnamon, and water. Bring the syrup to a boil, stirring constantly to dissolve sugar, then remove from heat.
3. Unroll pie crusts, press one into a 9-inch pie dish, and place the apples into the crust. Unroll the second crust on a work surface, and cut into about 8 1-inch wide strips. Criss-cross the strips over the apples, or weave into a lattice crust. Crimp the bottom crust over the lattice strips with your fingers. Spoon caramel sauce over pie, covering lattice portion of top crust; let remaining sauce drizzle through the crust.
4. Bake in preheated oven for 15 minutes. Reduce heat to 350 degrees F (175 degrees C), and bake until the crust is golden brown, the caramel on the top crust is set, and the apple filling is bubbling, 35 to 40 more minutes. Allow to cool completely before slicing.

CHOCOLATE CHESS PIE

Servings: 8 | Prep: 15m | Cooks: 40m | Total: 55m

NUTRITION FACTS

Calories: 357 | Carbohydrates: 50.8g | Fat: 16.1g | Protein: 4.6g | Cholesterol: 67mg

INGREDIENTS

- 1 1/2 cups white sugar
- 1/4 cup melted butter
- 3 tablespoons unsweetened cocoa powder
- 1 teaspoon vanilla extract
- 2 eggs
- 1 (9 inch) unbaked pie crust

1 (5 ounce) can evaporated milk

DIRECTIONS

1. Preheat oven to 350 degrees F (175 degrees C).
2. Mix sugar and cocoa together. Beat the eggs then add to the cocoa mixture. Beat in the milk, butter and vanilla.
3. Pour mixture into 9 inch unbaked pie shell and bake at 350 degrees F (175 degrees C) for 45 minutes or until set. Let cool before slicing.

GLAZED APPLE CREAM PIE

Servings: 8 | Prep: 15m | Cooks: 45m | Total: 3h | Additional: 2h

NUTRITION FACTS

Calories: 480 | Carbohydrates: 51.1g | Fat: 29.4g | Protein: 4.3g | Cholesterol: 41mg

INGREDIENTS

- 1/2 cup white sugar
- 1 tablespoon all-purpose flour
- 1/2 cup milk
- 1/4 teaspoon ground cinnamon
- 1/2 cup heavy cream
- 1 (15 ounce) package pastry for double-crust pie
- 1/4 cup butter
- 1/2 cup confectioners' sugar
- 2 tablespoons cornstarch
- 1 tablespoon milk
- 2 tablespoons milk
- 1/4 teaspoon vanilla extract
- 1 teaspoon vanilla extract
- 1 tablespoon butter, softened

2 tart apples - peeled, cored and sliced

DIRECTIONS

1. In a medium saucepan over medium heat, combine 1/2 cup sugar, 1/2 cup milk, 1/2 cup cream, and 1/4 cup butter. Heat until butter is melted, stirring occasionally. In a small bowl, whisk together the cornstarch, 2 tablespoons milk, and vanilla; stir into saucepan. Cook until thickened, stirring constantly. Remove from heat, and set aside to cool slightly.
2. Preheat oven to 400 degrees F (200 degrees C). In a medium bowl, combine the apples, flour, and cinnamon. Mix well.
3. Line a 9 inch pie pan with pie dough. Pour thickened filling mixture into pastry-lined pie pan. Arrange apple mixture evenly over filling. Top with second crust, seal and flute the edges. Cut slits in top crust.
4. Bake for 30 to 40 minutes, or until crust is golden brown and apples are tender. Cool for at least 30 minutes.
5. In small bowl, combine confectioners' sugar, 1 tablespoon milk, 1/4 teaspoon vanilla, and 1 tablespoon softened butter. Blend until smooth; pour evenly over warm pie. Refrigerate for AT LEAST 1 1/2 hours before serving (longer is better).

DOUBLE CHOCOLATE PIE

Servings: 8 | Prep: 10m | Cooks: 40m | Total: 4h50m | Additional: 4h

NUTRITION FACTS

Calories: 434 | Carbohydrates: 67g | Fat: 17.6g | Protein: 6.6g | Cholesterol: 110mg

INGREDIENTS

- 1 (9 inch) pie crust, baked
- 3/4 cup semisweet chocolate chips
- 1 1/2 cups white sugar
- 2 (1 ounce) squares unsweetened chocolate, chopped
- 1/3 cup cornstarch
- 4 egg yolks, beaten
- 1/2 teaspoon salt
- 1 tablespoon vanilla extract

3 cups milk

DIRECTIONS

1. Combine sugar, cornstarch, and salt in a 2-quart saucepan. Stir in milk gradually. Add chocolate chips and unsweetened chocolate. Place over medium heat, stirring constantly, until mixture thickens and boils. Boil and stir 1 minute.
2. Place egg yolks in a medium heatproof bowl. Gradually pour half of chocolate mixture into egg yolks, whisking constantly.
3. Whisk egg yolk mixture back into mixture in saucepan. Place over medium heat and bring back to a boil, stirring constantly. Boil and stir 1 minute. Remove from heat; stir in vanilla extract.
4. Pour mixture into baked pie shell. Press a layer of plastic wrap onto filling. Refrigerate at least 4 hours but no longer than 48 hours. Remove plastic wrap before serving and top with whipped topping.

HONEY CRUNCH PECAN PIE

Servings: 8 | Prep: 30m | Cooks: 1h | Total: 2h50m | Additional: 1h20m

NUTRITION FACTS

Calories: 848 | Carbohydrates: 88.8g | Fat: 53.6g | Protein: 9.6g | Cholesterol: 112mg

INGREDIENTS

- 2 cups all-purpose flour
- 1 cup light corn syrup

- 1 teaspoon salt
- 2 tablespoons butter, melted
- 3/4 cup shortening
- 1 teaspoon vanilla extract
- 6 tablespoons cold water
- 1 cup chopped pecans
- 1 teaspoon distilled white vinegar
- 1 tablespoon bourbon (optional)
- 4 eggs, lightly beaten
- 1/3 cup packed brown sugar
- 1/4 cup packed brown sugar
- 3 tablespoons butter
- 1/4 cup white sugar
- 3 tablespoons honey
- 1/2 teaspoon salt

1 1/2 cups pecan halves**DIRECTIONS**

1. Preheat oven to 350 degrees F (175 degrees C).
2. To Make Crust: In a medium bowl, mix together flour and 1 teaspoon salt. Cut in shortening until mixture is crumbly. Gradually add water and vinegar. Cut together until mixture will hold together. Press dough into a ball and flour each side lightly. Wrap in plastic and chill for 20 minutes. Roll out between wax paper into a circle 1/8 inch thick and press into 9 inch pie pan.
3. To Make Filling: In a large bowl, combine eggs, 1/4 cup brown sugar, white sugar, 1/2 teaspoon salt, corn syrup, melted butter, vanilla extract, and chopped pecans. Add bourbon if desired. Mix well. Spoon mixture into unbaked pie shell.
4. Bake in preheated oven for 15 minutes. Remove and cover edges of pastry with aluminum foil. Return to oven for 20 minutes.
5. To Make Topping: Combine 1/3 cup brown sugar, butter or margarine, and honey in a medium saucepan. Cook over low heat, stirring occasionally, until sugar dissolves - about 2 minutes. Add pecans. Stir just until coated. Spoon topping evenly over pie.
6. Keep foil on edges of pastry and return pie to oven for an additional 10 to 20 minutes, until topping is bubbly and golden brown. Cool to room temperature before serving.

KEY LIME PIE

Servings: 8 | Prep: 15m | Cooks: 15m | Total: 4h30m | Additional: 4h

NUTRITION FACTS

Calories: 420 | Carbohydrates: 42.7g | Fat: 25.4g | Protein: 7.8g | Cholesterol: 146mg

INGREDIENTS

- 1 cup graham cracker crumbs
- 1 (14 ounce) can sweetened condensed milk
- 3 tablespoons white sugar
- 1 pinch salt
- 5 tablespoons butter, melted
- 1 pinch cream of tartar
- 3 eggs
- 1 cup heavy whipping cream
- 1/2 cup key lime juice

1 lime, sliced **DIRECTIONS**

1. Preheat oven to 325 degrees F (165 degrees C). Mix graham cracker crumbs with sugar and melted butter. Press into 9 inch pie plate and bake for 5 minutes. Remove from oven and let cool.
2. Separate 2 of the eggs, placing the two egg whites into a mixing bowl. Reserve the yolks in another bowl.
3. To the yolks, add one whole egg, lime juice and sweetened condensed milk. Whisk until smooth. With clean mixer blades or a whisk attachment, beat the egg whites with salt and cream of tartar until stiff, but not dry. Fold whites into filling mixture. Pour filling into partially baked crust.
4. Bake in preheated 325 degrees F (165 degrees C) for 10 to 15 minutes or until set. Let cool at room temperature, then freeze 4 hours to overnight. Just before serving, whip cream to form stiff peaks. Serve decorated with whipped cream and lime slices.

PEACH-A-BERRY PIE

Servings: 8 | Prep: 25m | Cooks: 45m | Total: 1h25m | Additional: 15m

NUTRITION FACTS

Calories: 301 | Carbohydrates: 44.1g | Fat: 13.4g | Protein: 1.9g | Cholesterol: 8mg

INGREDIENTS

- 4 cups fresh peaches - peeled, pitted, and sliced
- 1 teaspoon ground cinnamon
- 1 cup fresh raspberries
- 2 (9 inch) pie crusts
- 3/4 cup white sugar
- 2 tablespoons butter, softened and cut into pieces
- 3 tablespoons all-purpose flour

1 tablespoon coarse granulated sugar**DIRECTIONS**

1. Preheat oven to 400 degrees F (200 degrees C).

2. Place peaches and berries in a colander for about 15 minutes to drain any excess fluid , then transfer to a large bowl. Gently toss with sugar, flour, and cinnamon. Transfer to a pie crust. Dot with butter, and top with remaining crust. Cut vents in top crust, and sprinkle with coarse sugar.
3. Bake 45 minutes in the preheated oven, until crust is golden brown.

PUMPKIN DESSERT
Servings: 18 | Prep: 10m | Cooks: 50m | Total: 1h

NUTRITION FACTS

Calories: 292 | Carbohydrates: 39.1g | Fat: 14.1g | Protein: 4.6g | Cholesterol: 58mg

INGREDIENTS

- 1 (18.25 ounce) package yellow cake mix
- 3 eggs
- 1/3 cup butter, melted
- 2 tablespoons pumpkin pie spice
- 1 egg
- 1/4 cup butter, chilled
- 1 (29 ounce) can pumpkin
- 1/2 cup white sugar
- 1/2 cup brown sugar
- 3/4 cup chopped walnuts

2/3 cup milk

DIRECTIONS

1. Preheat oven to 350 degrees F (175 degrees C) and lightly grease a 9x13 inch baking dish.
2. Set aside 1 cup of cake mix. Combine remaining cake mix with melted butter and 1 egg and mix until well blended; spread mixture in the bottom of the prepared baking dish.
3. In a large bowl combine pumpkin, brown sugar, milk, 3 eggs and pumpkin pie spice; mix well and pour this mixture over cake mix mixture in baking dish.
4. In a small bowl with a pastry blender, or in a food processor, combine chilled butter and white sugar with reserved cake mix until mixture resembles coarse crumbs. Sprinkle over pumpkin mixture. Sprinkle chopped walnuts over all.

Bake 45 to 50 minutes, until top is golden. # EASY PUMPKIN PIE SQUARES
Servings: 24 | Prep: 20m | Cooks: 35m | Total: 55m

NUTRITION FACTS

Calories: 134 | Carbohydrates: 18.9g | Fat: 5.7g | Protein: 2.7g | Cholesterol: 30mg

INGREDIENTS

- 1/2 cup butter, softened
- 1 (15 ounce) can pumpkin
- 1/2 cup brown sugar
- 1 (12 fluid ounce) can evaporated milk
- 1 cup all-purpose flour
- 1/2 teaspoon salt
- 1/2 cup rolled oats
- 1 teaspoon ground cinnamon
- 2 eggs
- 1/2 teaspoon ground ginger
- 3/4 cup white sugar

1/4 teaspoon ground cloves **DIRECTIONS**

1. Preheat oven to 350 degrees F (175 degrees C).
2. In a medium bowl, cream together butter and brown sugar. Mix in flour. Fold in oats. Press into a 9x13 inch baking dish.
3. Bake in preheated oven 15 minutes, until set.
4. In a large bowl, beat eggs with white sugar. Beat in pumpkin and evaporated milk. Mix in salt, cinnamon, ginger and cloves. Pour over baked crust.
5. Bake in preheated oven 20 minutes, until set. Let cool before cutting into squares.

RHUBARB SOUR CREAM PIE
Servings: 8 | Prep: 15m | Cooks: 55m | Total: 1h10m

NUTRITION FACTS

Calories: 493 | Carbohydrates: 75.2g | Fat: 20.1g | Protein: 5g | Cholesterol: 51mg

INGREDIENTS

- 1 (9 inch) unbaked pie crust
- 1/3 cup all-purpose flour
- 4 cups chopped fresh rhubarb
- 1/2 cup all-purpose flour
- 1 egg
- 1/2 cup brown sugar
- 1 1/2 cups white sugar
- 1/4 cup butter, melted

1 cup sour cream

DIRECTIONS

1. Preheat the oven to 450 degrees F (220 degrees C).
2. Press the pie crust into a 9 inch pie pan. Spread rhubarb in an even layer in the bottom of the crust. In a medium bowl, whisk together the egg, white sugar, sour cream and 1/3 cup of flour until smooth. Pour over the rhubarb.
3. In a small bowl, mix together 1/2 cup of flour and brown sugar. Stir in melted butter until the mixture is crumbly. Sprinkle over the top of the pie.
4. Bake for 15 minutes in the preheated oven, then reduce the heat to 350 degrees F (175 degrees C). Continue to bake for 40 minutes, or until the edges have puffed, and the topping is golden. The center may still be slightly jiggly. Cool completely before slicing and serving.

NO FAIL PIE CRUST
Servings: 24 | Prep: 10m | Cooks: 0m | Total: 10m

NUTRITION FACTS

Calories: 126 | Carbohydrates: 10g | Fat: 8.9g | Protein: 1.6g | Cholesterol: 8mg

INGREDIENTS

- 2 1/2 cups all-purpose flour
- 1 egg
- 1 cup shortening
- 1/4 cup cold water
- 1/4 teaspoon salt

1 tablespoon distilled white vinegar**DIRECTIONS**

1. Combine flour and salt in a large bowl. Cut in shortening until it resembles coarse crumbs.
2. Mix egg, water, and vinegar together in a separate bowl. Pour into flour all at once and blend with a fork until dough forms into a ball. Divide into 3 equal-sized rounds.
3. Wrap with plastic and chill in a refrigerator until ready to prepare.

EASY SWEDISH APPLE PIE
Servings: 8 | Prep: 20m | Cooks: 45m | Total: 1h5m

NUTRITION FACTS

Calories: 359 | Carbohydrates: 49.3g | Fat: 18g | Protein: 2.8g | Cholesterol: 69mg

INGREDIENTS

- 1 1/2 pounds Granny Smith apples - peeled, cored and sliced
- 1 teaspoon cinnamon
- 1 tablespoon sugar
- 3/4 cup melted butter
- 1 cup sugar
- 1 egg

1 cup flour

DIRECTIONS

1. Preheat oven to 350 degrees F (175 degrees C).
2. Toss apples with 1 tablespoon of sugar, and pour them into a pie plate. Thoroughly mix together 1 cup of sugar with the flour, cinnamon, butter, and egg. Spread this evenly over the top of the pie.
3. Bake in preheated oven until the apples have cooked and the topping is golden brown, about 40 to 45 minutes.

COCONUT (HAUPIA) AND CHOCOLATE PIE
Servings: 8 | Prep: 25m | Cooks: 20m | Total: 1h45m | Additional: 1h

NUTRITION FACTS

Calories: 654 | Carbohydrates: 69.9g | Fat: 42.5g | Protein: 5g | Cholesterol: 64mg

INGREDIENTS

- 1 (9 inch) unbaked pie crust
- 1/2 cup cornstarch
- 1 cup milk
- 1 1/4 cups semi-sweet chocolate chips
- 1 (14 ounce) can coconut milk
- 1 1/2 cups heavy cream
- 1 cup white sugar
- 1/4 cup white sugar

1 cup water**DIRECTIONS**

1. Preheat oven to 350 degrees F (175 degrees C). Bake crust for 15 minutes, or until golden brown. Set aside to cool.
2. In a medium saucepan, whisk together milk, coconut milk and 1 cup sugar. In a separate bowl, dissolve the cornstarch in water. Bring coconut mixture to a boil. Reduce to simmer and slowly whisk in the cornstarch. Continue stirring mixture over low heat until thickened, about 3 minutes.
3. In a glass bowl, microwave chocolate chips for 1 minute or until melted. Divide the coconut pudding evenly into two bowls. Mix chocolate into one portion. Spread on the bottom of the pie crust. Pour

the remaining portion of pudding on top of the chocolate and spread smooth. Refrigerate for about an hour.

4. Whip cream with 1/4 cup sugar until stiff peaks form. Layer the cream on pie; if desired garnish with chocolate shavings.

DOUBLE LAYER CHOCOLATE PEANUT BUTTER PIE
Servings: 8 | Prep: 20m | Cooks: 4h | Total: 4h20m | Additional: 4h

NUTRITION FACTS

Calories: 648 | Carbohydrates: 65.5g | Fat: 37.6g | Protein: 14g | Cholesterol: 21mg

INGREDIENTS

- 1/2 (8 ounce) package cream cheese, softened
- 1 (9 inch) prepared graham cracker crust
- 1 tablespoon white sugar
- 2 (3.9 ounce) packages instant chocolate pudding mix
- 1 tablespoon cold milk
- 2 cups cold milk
- 1 cup peanut butter
- 4 peanut butter cups, cut into 1/2 inch pieces

1 (8 ounce) container frozen whipped topping, thawed

DIRECTIONS

1. In a large bowl, mix cream cheese, sugar, 1 tablespoon milk and peanut butter until smooth. Gently stir in 1 1/2 cups of whipped topping. Spread mixture on bottom of pie crust.
2. In a second bowl, stir pudding mix with 2 cups milk until thick. Immediately stir in remaining whipped topping. Spread mixture over peanut butter layer.
3. Scatter peanut butter cups over top of pie. Cover and refrigerate for 4 hours.

PEAR PIE
Servings: 8 | Prep: 15m | Cooks: 1h | Total: 1h15m

NUTRITION FACTS

Calories: 328 | Carbohydrates: 46.6g | Fat: 14.6g | Protein: 3.6g | Cholesterol: 62mg

INGREDIENTS

- 1 (9 inch) unbaked pie crust
- 1/4 cup all-purpose flour

- 2 pears - peeled, cored and cut in half
- 1 tablespoon vanilla extract
- 1 cup white sugar
- 2 eggs, beaten

1/4 cup butter

DIRECTIONS

1. Preheat the oven to 350 degrees F (175 degrees C).
2. Press the pie pastry into the bottom and up the sides of a 9 inch pie plate. Flute the edges. Place the pear halves cut side down in the pie crust with the small ends toward the center.
3. In a medium bowl, mix the butter and sugar together until smooth, then beat in the eggs one at a time until light and fluffy. Stir in flour and vanilla. Pour over the top of the pears.
4. Bake for 1 hour in the preheated oven, until pears are soft and custard is set in the center. Cool completely before slicing and serving.

PHOENICIAN'S KEY LIME PIE

Servings: 8 | Prep: 20m | Cooks: 25m | Total: 10h45m | Additional: 10m

NUTRITION FACTS

Calories: 456 | Carbohydrates: 47.3g | Fat: 26.9g | Protein: 8.7g | Cholesterol: 165mg

INGREDIENTS

- 2/3 cup toasted slivered almonds
- 4 egg yolks
- 1 cup graham cracker crumbs
- 1 (14 ounce) can sweetened condensed milk
- 1/4 cup white sugar
- 1/2 cup key lime juice
- 1 pinch salt
- 3/4 cup cold heavy cream
- 1/4 cup butter, melted

1/2 teaspoon grated lime zest**DIRECTIONS**

1. Preheat an oven to 350 degrees F (175 degrees C).
2. Pulse the almonds in a food processor until finely ground. Combine the almonds with the graham cracker crumbs, sugar, and salt. Pour in the melted butter and mix until evenly moistened. Press into a 9-inch pie plate.
3. Bake the crust in the preheated oven until golden brown, 10 to 13 minutes.

4. While the crust is baking, beat the egg yolks in a bowl with the condensed milk, cream, and lime zest. Whisk in the lime juice a little at a time to thicken the custard. Pour the custard into the pie crust and return to the oven.
5. Bake in the oven for 15 minutes to help the custard begin to set. Cool to room temperature on a wire rack before covering loosely with plastic wrap and refrigerating overnight.

SUNDAY'S APPLE PIE
Servings: 8 | Prep: 45m | Cooks: 50m | Total: 1h35m

NUTRITION FACTS

Calories: 376 | Carbohydrates: 49.3g | Fat: 19.5g | Protein: 3.3g | Cholesterol: 11mg

INGREDIENTS

- 1 recipe pastry for a 9 inch double crust pie
- 2 teaspoons ground cinnamon
- 6 tart apples - peeled, cored and sliced
- 2 tablespoons all-purpose flour
- 1/2 cup white sugar

3 tablespoons butter, divided **DIRECTIONS**

1. Preheat oven to 350 degrees F (175 degrees C). Place a baking sheet on an oven rack.
2. Place sliced apples in a large bowl. In a small bowl, combine sugar, cinnamon, and flour. Stir well and pour mixture over apples. Cut half of butter into small pieces and add to apples. Toss apples until thoroughly coated.
3. Roll out pastry to fit an 8- or 9-inch pie plate. Roll out top crust and set aside. Pour apples into pastry-lined pie pan.
4. Dot apples with remaining butter. Place second pastry on top. Seal edges and cut steam vents in top crust.
5. Bake in preheated oven on the baking sheet until apple filling is bubbly and crust is golden brown, 50 minutes to 1 hour.

BLACKBERRY AND BLUEBERRY PIE
Servings: 8 | Prep: 30m | Cooks: 45m | Total: 1h45m | Additional: 30m

NUTRITION FACTS

Calories: 436 | Carbohydrates: 59.9g | Fat: 20.7g | Protein: 4.7g | Cholesterol: 8mg

INGREDIENTS

- 2/3 cup shortening, chilled

- 1/2 teaspoon ground cinnamon
- 2 cups all-purpose flour
- 4 cups fresh blueberries
- 1 teaspoon salt
- 1 1/2 cups fresh blackberries
- 5 tablespoons cold water
- 1 tablespoon lemon juice
- 3/4 cup white sugar
- 2 tablespoons butter

1/3 cup all-purpose flour

DIRECTIONS

1. Cut shortening into 2 cups flour and salt until the shortening is the size of small peas. Sprinkle in water 1 tablespoon at a time until flour is moistened. Gather into a ball, wrap with plastic, and refrigerate at least 30 minutes. Divide the dough in half and roll out half on a lightly floured board. Line a 9-inch pie dish with the pastry. Roll out the top crust and set aside.
2. Preheat oven to 425 degrees F (220 degrees C).
3. Mix sugar, 1/3 cup flour, and cinnamon. Stir in berries to coat. Pour the filling into the pastry-lined pan. Sprinkle with lemon juice and dot with butter. Cover with top crust; cut slits in the top to vent the steam. Seal the crust and flute the edges.
4. Cover the edges of the crust with foil to prevent over-browning. Bake in the preheated oven until the crust is golden brown and the juices are bubbling, about 45 minutes. Remove foil during the last 12 minutes of baking.

PUMPKIN MAPLE PIE SUPREME

Servings: 8 | Prep: 30m | Cooks: 2h | Total: 2h30m

NUTRITION FACTS

Calories: 356 | Carbohydrates: 54.5g | Fat: 14g | Protein: 5.5g | Cholesterol: 84mg

INGREDIENTS

- 1 small sugar pumpkin
- 1/2 teaspoon salt
- 3/4 cup packed brown sugar
- 2/3 cup real maple syrup
- 1 1/4 teaspoons ground cinnamon
- 1 1/4 cups half-and-half cream
- 1 teaspoon ground ginger
- 1 teaspoon all-purpose flour
- 1 teaspoon ground nutmeg

- 3 eggs
- 1/4 teaspoon ground cloves
- 1 (9 inch) unbaked pie shell

1/8 teaspoon ground allspice

DIRECTIONS

1. Preheat oven to 375 degrees F (190 degrees C)
2. Cut up pumpkin, and remove seeds. Place in large baking pan, and cover with foil or lid. Bake for 1 hour, or until very tender. Remove from oven, and set aside to cool. Reduce oven temperature to 350 degrees F (175 degrees C).
3. Scrape pumpkin into a food processor; puree until smooth. Measure 1 1/2 cups pumpkin puree. In a large bowl, mix together 1 1/2 cups pumpkin, brown sugar, cinnamon, ginger, nutmeg, cloves, allspice, and salt. Stir in maple syrup, half-and-half, and flour. Mix in eggs one at a time. Pour filling into unbaked pie shell.
4. Bake at 350 degrees F (175 degrees C) for 1 hour, or until center is set.

BETTER THAN PUMPKIN PIE
Servings: 8 | Prep: 20m | Cooks: 50m | Total: 1h10m

NUTRITION FACTS

Calories: 249 | Carbohydrates: 36.2g | Fat: 10.2g | Protein: 4.2g | Cholesterol: 32mg

INGREDIENTS

- 1 1/2 cups peeled and cubed butternut squash
- 1 pinch ground allspice
- 1 cup lightly packed brown sugar
- 1 pinch ground cloves
- 1 tablespoon cornstarch
- 1 pinch ground ginger
- 1 egg, beaten
- 1 pinch ground nutmeg
- 1 cup evaporated milk
- 1 (9 inch) unbaked pie shell

1 teaspoon ground cinnamon

DIRECTIONS

1. Place squash in a saucepan with enough water to cover. Bring to a boil, and simmer over medium heat until tender, about 15 minutes. Drain, and cool.
2. Preheat oven to 350 degrees F (175 degrees C).

3. In a blender or food processor, combine butternut squash, brown sugar, cornstarch, egg, milk, cinnamon, allspice, cloves, ginger, and nutmeg. Process until smooth. Pour into the unbaked pie shell.
4. Bake in preheated oven for 50 minutes, or until a table knife comes out clean when inserted in the center.

RASPBERRY SOUR CREAM PIE
Servings: 16 | Prep: 20m | Cooks: 40m | Total: 2h | Additional: 1h

NUTRITION FACTS

Calories: 307 | Carbohydrates: 36.1g | Fat: 16.8g | Protein: 4.1g | Cholesterol: 39mg

INGREDIENTS

- 2 (9 inch) unbaked pie crusts
- 1/3 cup all-purpose flour
- 2 eggs
- 3 cups raspberries
- 1 1/3 cups sour cream
- 1/2 cup brown sugar
- 1 teaspoon vanilla extract
- 1/2 cup all-purpose flour
- 1 cup white sugar
- 1/2 cup chopped walnuts
- 1 pinch salt

1/4 cup butter, chilled **DIRECTIONS**

1. Preheat oven to 400 degrees F (200 degrees C).
2. In a large bowl, beat eggs until light and lemon colored. Whisk in sour cream and vanilla. In a separate bowl, mix sugar, flour and salt together. Stir into egg mixture. Gently fold in raspberries. Pour filling into 2 unbaked pie crusts.
3. Bake the pies without the topping in the preheated oven for 30 to 35 minutes, or until the center begins to set.
4. While pies bake, make the topping: In a medium bowl, mix together brown sugar, flour and chopped nuts. Cut in butter until crumbly. Set aside.
5. Sprinkle pies with topping and return to oven for 10 to 15 minutes, or until topping is golden brown. Allow to cool before serving.

TART LEMON TRIANGLES
Servings: 8 | Prep: 35m | Cooks: 0m | Total: 35m

NUTRITION FACTS

Calories: 291 | Carbohydrates: 45.7g | Fat: 10.7g | Protein: 4.4g | Cholesterol: 93mg

INGREDIENTS

- 3/8 cup butter
- 1 tablespoon grated lemon zest
- 1/4 cup confectioners' sugar
- 1/4 cup lemon juice
- 1 cup all-purpose flour
- 3 tablespoons all-purpose flour
- 3 eggs
- 2 tablespoons confectioners' sugar for dusting

1 cup white sugar

DIRECTIONS

1. Preheat oven to 350 degrees F (175 degrees C).
2. Process butter, 1/4 cup confectioners' sugar and 1 cup flour in food processor 10 seconds, or blend with pastry blender. Pat dough evenly into 9 inch round pie plate.
3. Bake 12 to 15 minutes, until golden.
4. Combine eggs, white sugar, lemon zest, lemon juice and 3 tablespoons flour and mix until smooth; pour mixture over hot crust.

Bake 15 to 20 minutes more, until firm. Let cool completely in baking dish. Sprinkle with confectioners' sugar and cut into 12 triangles. # FRENCH SILK CHOCOLATE PIE

Servings: 10 | Prep: 50m | Cooks: 2h | Total: 2h50m | Additional: 2h

NUTRITION FACTS

Calories: 428 | Carbohydrates: 33.5g | Fat: 30.9g | Protein: 4.8g | Cholesterol: 130mg

INGREDIENTS

- 1 Pillsbury refrigerated pie crust, softened as directed on box
- 1/2 teaspoon vanilla
- 3 (1 ounce) squares Hershey's unsweetened chocolate, cut into pieces
- 4 pasteurized eggs or equivalent fat-free cholesterol-free egg product
- 1 cup LAND O LAKES butter, softened (do not use margarine)
- 1/2 cup sweetened whipped cream
- 1 cup sugar

Chocolate curls (optional) **DIRECTIONS**

1. Heat oven to 450 degrees F. Make pie crust as directed on box for One-Crust Baked Shell using 9-inch glass pie pan. Bake 9 to 11 minutes or until light golden brown. Cool completely, about 30 minutes.
2. In 1-quart saucepan, melt chocolate over low heat; cool. In small bowl with electric mixer, beat butter on medium speed until fluffy. Gradually beat in sugar until light and fluffy. Beat in cooled chocolate and vanilla until well blended.
3. Add eggs 1 at a time, beating on high speed 2 minutes after each addition; beat until mixture is smooth and fluffy. Pour into cooled baked shell. Refrigerate at least 2 hours before serving. Garnish with whipped cream and chocolate curls. Store in refrigerator.

CHERRY-BLUEBERRY PIE

Servings: 8 | Prep: 15m | Cooks: 45m | Total: 3h | Additional: 2h

NUTRITION FACTS

Calories: 409 | Carbohydrates: 62g | Fat: 6.4g | Protein: 3.9g | Cholesterol: 0mg

INGREDIENTS

- 1 (15 ounce) package refrigerated pie crusts
- 1 1/2 cups frozen blueberries
- 1/2 cup white sugar
- 1 egg white
- 2 tablespoons cornstarch
- 1 teaspoon water
- 1/4 teaspoon ground cinnamon
- 2 teaspoons sugar

1 (21 ounce) can cherry pie filling

DIRECTIONS

1. Preheat the oven to 425 degrees F (220 degrees C).
2. Press one of the pie crusts into a 9 inch pie plate. In a large bowl, stir together 1/2 cup of sugar, cornstarch and cinnamon. Stir in the cherry pie filling and blueberries. Spoon into the pie crust. Top with the second crust, and press the edges to seal. Flute edges, or press with the tines of a fork. In a cup, whisk together the egg white and water with a fork. Brush over the top of the pie, then sprinkle with 2 teaspoons of sugar.
3. Bake for 45 to 55 minutes in the preheated oven, or until crust is golden brown. Cover the edges of the crust with aluminum foil if they appear to be getting too dark. Cool for at least 2 hours to allow the filling to set before serving.

SMOOTH AND CREAMY PEANUT BUTTER PIE

Servings: 8 | Prep: 15m | Cooks: 3h | Total: 3h15m

NUTRITION FACTS

Calories: 527 | Carbohydrates: 48.5g | Fat: 35.2g | Protein: 8.8g | Cholesterol: 12mg

INGREDIENTS

- 3/4 cup creamy peanut butter
- 1 (12 ounce) container frozen whipped topping, thawed
- 1 (3 ounce) package cream cheese
- 1 (9 inch) prepared chocolate cookie crumb crust

1 1/4 cups confectioners' sugar

DIRECTIONS

1. In a large bowl, mix together peanut butter, cream cheese and sugar. Then stir whipped topping into peanut butter mixture. Whisk until smooth and no lumps remain.
2. Pour filling into pie crust and refrigerate for about 3 hours until pie is firm.

AUNT BEV'S FAMOUS APPLE PIE

Servings: 8 | Prep: 20m | Cooks: 50m | Total: 1h10m

NUTRITION FACTS

Calories: 616 | Carbohydrates: 84g | Fat: 30g | Protein: 4.3g | Cholesterol: 4mg

INGREDIENTS

- 7 tart apples, peeled and cored
- 1/2 teaspoon ground nutmeg
- 1 cup white sugar
- salt to taste
- 1 1/2 teaspoons ground cinnamon, or to taste
- 2 recipes unbaked pie shells
- 2 tablespoons all-purpose flour

1 tablespoon butter **DIRECTIONS**

1. Preheat oven to 400 degrees F (200 degrees C).
2. Cut the apples into 1/4 inch slices.
3. In a mixing bowl, combine sugar, cinnamon, flour, nutmeg (or apple pie spice), and salt; mix thoroughly. Pour the spice mix over the apples and stir until the apples are coated.

4. Line one crust in a 9 inch deep dish pie pan. Place the apples in the pie crust. Dot the apple filling evenly with butter. Fit the top crust over the apples. Press the crust down gently and cut 3 or 4 slits in the top crust to allow steam to escape while the pie bakes
5. Bake in the preheated oven 50 minutes, or until the crust is golden brown. Check the pie after the first 30 minutes of cooking: if the crust is already browned reduce the heat to 350 degrees F (175 degrees C) to allow the apples to cook without the crust burning.

MOCK COCONUT PIE (SPAGHETTI SQUASH PIE)
Servings: 8 | Prep: 20m | Cooks: 40m | Total: 1h

NUTRITION FACTS

Calories: 424 | Carbohydrates: 37.2g | Fat: 29.6g | Protein: 4.3g | Cholesterol: 146mg

INGREDIENTS

- 1 cup white sugar
- 3 cups cooked, shredded spaghetti squash
- 3 eggs
- 1 (9 inch) pie shell, baked
- 1/4 cup butter, melted
- 1 pinch ground nutmeg (optional)
- 1 tablespoon fresh lemon juice
- 1 pinch ground cinnamon (optional)
- 1 teaspoon vanilla extract

1 1/2 cups whipped cream for garnish (optional) **DIRECTIONS**

1. Preheat oven to 350 degrees F (175 degrees C).
2. Beat the sugar and eggs together in a mixing bowl until light and frothy. Beat in the butter, lemon juice, and vanilla until well blended. Stir in the spaghetti squash. Pour the mixture into the prebaked pie shell. If desired, dust the top with nutmeg and cinnamon.
3. Bake the pie in preheated oven until a knife inserted in the center comes out clean, 40 to 45 minutes. Cool on a rack before serving. Garnish with whipped cream, if desired.

CREAMY PUMPKIN PIE
Servings: 8 | Prep: 10m | Cooks: 55m | Total: 1h5m

NUTRITION FACTS

Calories: 319 | Carbohydrates: 44.4g | Fat: 13.1g | Protein: 7.4g | Cholesterol: 63mg

INGREDIENTS

- 4 cups fresh pumpkin, cooked and mashed
- 1/2 teaspoon ground ginger
- 1 (14 ounce) can sweetened condensed milk
- 1/2 teaspoon ground nutmeg
- 2 eggs
- 1/2 teaspoon salt
- 1 teaspoon ground cinnamon

1 (9 inch) deep dish pie crust**DIRECTIONS**

1. Preheat oven to 425 degrees F (220 degrees C.)
2. In a large bowl, combine pumpkin puree, sweetened condensed milk and eggs. Season with cinnamon, ginger, nutmeg and salt. Mix together with a wire whisk until thoroughly blended. Pour filling into pie crust.
3. Bake in preheated oven for 15 minutes. Reduce the heat to 350 degrees F (175 degrees C) and bake another 35 to 40 minutes or until a knife inserted comes out clean.

SUGAR CREAM PIE
Servings: 8 | Prep: 30m | Cooks: 30m | Total: 2h | Additional: 1h

NUTRITION FACTS

Calories: 336 | Carbohydrates: 33.3g | Fat: 21.6g | Protein: 2.8g | Cholesterol: 48mg

INGREDIENTS

- 1 (9 inch) pie crust, baked
- 2 1/4 cups half-and-half cream
- 4 tablespoons cornstarch
- 1 teaspoon vanilla extract
- 3/4 cup white sugar
- 2 tablespoons butter, melted
- 4 tablespoons butter, melted

1/2 teaspoon ground cinnamon **DIRECTIONS**

1. Mix cornstarch and sugar. Add 4 tablespoons butter and half and half. Cook over medium heat, stirring constantly, until mixture boils and becomes thick and creamy. Remove from heat and stir in the vanilla.
2. Preheat oven broiler to high.
3. Pour mixture into pie crust. Drizzle 2 tablespoons butter over top and sprinkle with cinnamon. Put under broiler until butter bubbles--watch it carefully as it doesn't take long. Refrigerate for at least 1 hour before serving.

PECAN TASSIES

Servings: 60 | Prep: 25m | Cooks: 15m | Total: 40m

NUTRITION FACTS

Calories: 166 | Carbohydrates: 16g | Fat: 10.8g | Protein: 1.9g | Cholesterol: 17mg

INGREDIENTS

- 2 cups margarine
- 3 tablespoons melted butter
- 4 (3 ounce) packages cream cheese
- 1/2 teaspoon vanilla extract
- 4 cups all-purpose flour
- 1 pinch salt
- 3 eggs
- 1 1/2 cups chopped pecans

2 1/2 cups packed brown sugar

DIRECTIONS

1. Preheat the oven to 350 degrees F (175 degrees C).
2. In a medium bowl, mix together the margarine and cream cheese until well blended. Beat in flour, 1 cup at a time, until the mixture forms a smooth dough. Roll into small balls, and press into the bottoms and sides of tart pans or mini muffin pans.
3. In another bowl, mix together the eggs, brown sugar, butter, vanilla, and salt. Stir in the pecans. Use a spoon to fill each of the crusts 2/3 full with the filling mixture.
4. Bake for 15 to 18 minutes in the preheated oven, until shell is light brown, and the filling has puffed up. Cool, and carefully remove from pans.

HONG KONG STYLE EGG TARTS

Servings: 12 | Prep: 25m | Cooks: 20m | Total: 45m

NUTRITION FACTS

Calories: 421 | Carbohydrates: 47.8g | Fat: 21.4g | Protein: 10.1g | Cholesterol: 202mg

INGREDIENTS

- 1 cup confectioners' sugar
- 2/3 cup white sugar
- 3 cups all-purpose flour
- 1 1/2 cups water

- 1 cup butter
- 9 eggs, beaten
- 1 egg, beaten
- 1 dash vanilla extract
- 1 dash vanilla extract

1 cup evaporated milk **DIRECTIONS**

1. In a medium bowl, mix together the confectioners' sugar and flour. Mix in butter with a fork until it is in small crumbs. Stir in the egg and vanilla until the mixture forms a dough. The texture should be slightly moist. Add more butter if it is too dry, or more flour, if the dough seems greasy. Shape dough into 1 1/2 inch balls, and press the balls into tart molds so that it covers the bottom, and goes up higher than the sides. Use 2 fingers to shape the edge into an A shape.
2. Preheat the oven to 450 degrees F (230 degrees C). Combine the white sugar and water in a medium saucepan, and bring to a boil. Cook until the sugar is dissolved, remove from heat and cool to room temperature. Strain the eggs through a sieve, and whisk into the sugar mixture. Stir in the evaporated milk and vanilla. Strain the filling through a sieve, and fill the tart shells.
3. Bake for 15 to 20 minutes in the preheated oven, until golden brown, and the filling is puffed up a little bit.

SWEET POTATO PIE
Servings: 16 | Prep: 20m | Cooks: 1h | Total: 1h20m

NUTRITION FACTS

Calories: 371 | Carbohydrates: 53.8g | Fat: 15.4g | Protein: 5.2g | Cholesterol: 65mg

INGREDIENTS

- 3 large sweet potatoes
- 1/2 teaspoon ground nutmeg
- 1/2 cup butter, softened
- 4 eggs, beaten
- 1 tablespoon vanilla extract
- 3/4 cup evaporated milk
- 2 cups sugar, or more to taste

2 (9 inch) unbaked pie shells **DIRECTIONS**

1. Bring a large pot of water to a boil. Add sweet potatoes and cook until tender but still firm, about 30 minutes. Drain, cool, peel and mash. Preheat oven to 350 degrees F (175 degrees C).
2. In a large bowl, combine sweet potatoes, butter, sugar, vanilla and nutmeg. In a small bowl, whisk together the eggs and milk and blend into the sweet potato mixture.
3. Pour into pie shells and bake in preheated oven for 60 minutes, or until done.

APPLE BUTTER PUMPKIN PIE
Servings: 8 | Prep: 30m | Cooks: 1h | Total: 1h30m

NUTRITION FACTS

Calories: 413 | Carbohydrates: 49.5g | Fat: 21.3g | Protein: 7.5g | Cholesterol: 90mg

INGREDIENTS

- 1 cup canned pumpkin puree
- 1 cup evaporated milk
- 1 cup apple butter
- 1 (9 inch) unbaked deep dish pie crust
- 1/4 cup dark brown sugar
- 3 tablespoons butter
- 1/2 teaspoon ground cinnamon
- 1/2 cup all-purpose flour
- 1/2 teaspoon ground nutmeg
- 1/3 cup dark brown sugar
- 1/4 teaspoon salt
- 1/2 cup chopped pecans

3 eggs, beaten

DIRECTIONS

1. Preheat oven to 350 degrees F (175 degrees C).
2. In a large bowl, combine pumpkin, apple butter, 1/4 cup brown sugar, cinnamon, nutmeg, and salt. Stir in eggs and evaporated milk. Pour into prepared pie shell.
3. Bake in preheated oven for 50 to 60 minutes, or until a knife inserted 2 inches from the center comes out clean. Sprinkle streusel topping over the pie, and bake for an additional 15 minutes.
4. To make the streusel topping: In a small bowl, combine butter, flour, and 1/3 cup brown sugar. Stir until mixture resembles coarse crumbs. Stir in pecans.

NO ROLL PIE CRUST
Servings: 8 | Prep: 15m | Cooks: 8m | Total: 23m

NUTRITION FACTS

Calories: 213 | Carbohydrates: 18.6g | Fat: 14.3g | Protein: 2.5g | Cholesterol: <1mg

INGREDIENTS

- 1 1/2 cups all-purpose flour

- 1/2 cup canola oil
- 1 teaspoon white sugar
- 2 tablespoons milk

1/2 teaspoon salt

DIRECTIONS

1. In a 9 inch pie plate, sift flour, sugar and salt. make a well in the center and pour in oil and milk. Mix with a fork, then press into the bottom and sides of pie plate.
2. To bake: Preheat oven to 450 degrees F (230 degrees C.) Bake for 8 to 10 minutes, or until golden brown.

BIG GUY STRAWBERRY PIE

Servings: 8 | Prep: 30m | Cooks: 30m | Total: 4h | Additional: 3h

NUTRITION FACTS

Calories: 277 | Carbohydrates: 41.5g | Fat: 11.9g | Protein: 2.3g | Cholesterol: 31mg

INGREDIENTS

- 1 cup water
- 1 cup all-purpose flour
- 3/4 cup white sugar
- 1/2 cup butter
- 1/4 teaspoon salt
- 3 tablespoons confectioners' sugar
- 2 tablespoons cornstarch
- 1 teaspoon vanilla extract
- 1/4 teaspoon red food coloring (optional)

1 quart fresh strawberries, hulled **DIRECTIONS**

1. In a saucepan, combine water, white sugar, salt, cornstarch and food coloring (optional). Bring to a boil, and cook for about 5 minutes or until thickened. Set aside to cool. Preheat oven to 350 degrees F (175 degrees C.)
2. In a large bowl, combine flour, confectioners' sugar, and vanilla. Cut in butter until the mixture resembles small crumbs. Press into a 9-inch pie pan. Prick all over with a fork and bake in the preheated oven for 8 to 10 minutes, or until lightly browned.
3. When crust is cool, place berries in the shell, and pour the thickened mixture over the top. Chill in refrigerator.

CREAM CHEESE TART SHELLS

Servings: 24 | Prep: 40m | Cooks: 20m | Total: 2h | Additional: 1h

NUTRITION FACTS

Calories: 65 | Carbohydrates: 4.1g | Fat: 5.1g | Protein: 0.8g | Cholesterol: 14mg

INGREDIENTS

- 3 ounces cream cheese, softened
- 1/2 cup butter, softened

1 cup all-purpose flour

DIRECTIONS

1. Blend cream cheese and butter or margarine. Stir in flour just until blended. Chill about 1 hour. This can be made ahead and chilled for up to 24 hours.
2. Preheat oven to 325 degrees F (165 degrees C).
3. Shape dough into 24 one-inch balls and press into ungreased 1 1/2 inch muffin cups (mini-muffin size) to make a shallow shell. Fill with your favorite filling and bake for 20 minutes, or until the crust is light brown.

VANILLA AND CHOCOLATE DELIGHT

Servings: 18 | Prep: 20m | Cooks: 25m | Total: 45m

NUTRITION FACTS

Calories: 350 | Carbohydrates: 34g | Fat: 22.6g | Protein: 4.4g | Cholesterol: 32mg

INGREDIENTS

- 1 cup finely chopped pecans
- 1 (16 ounce) container frozen whipped topping, thawed, divided
- 1 cup all-purpose flour
- 3 cups milk
- 1/2 cup butter, melted
- 1 (3.9 ounce) package instant chocolate pudding mix
- 1 (8 ounce) package cream cheese, softened
- 1 (3.4 ounce) package instant vanilla pudding mix
- 1 cup confectioners' sugar
- 2 (1.45 ounce) bars milk chocolate with crispy rice, crumbled

DIRECTIONS

1. Preheat oven to 400 degrees F (200 degrees C). In a medium mixing bowl, combine pecans, flour, and butter. Press into a 9x13 inch pan. Bake for 25 minutes. Allow to cool.
2. In a large bowl, beat together cream cheese and confectioners' sugar until smooth. Fold in half of the whipped topping. Spread on top of cooled crust.

In a large bowl, combine milk, chocolate pudding mix, and vanilla pudding mix. Beat until thick. Pour over cream cheese layer. Top with remaining whipped topping, and sprinkle with crushed chocolate bars.

STRAWBERRY RHUBARB CUSTARD PIE

Servings: 8 | Prep: 20m | Cooks: 1h | Total: 2h20m

NUTRITION FACTS

Calories: 342| Carbohydrates: 57.4g | Fat: 11.1g | Protein: 4.8g | Cholesterol: 74mg

INGREDIENTS

- 1 (9 inch) unbaked pie crust (see footnote for recipe link)
- 3 tablespoons all-purpose flour
- 3 cups rhubarb, sliced 1/4-inch thick
- 1/4 teaspoon freshly grated nutmeg
- 1 cup fresh strawberries, quartered
- 1 tablespoon butter, diced
- 3 large eggs
- 2 tablespoons strawberry jam
- 1 1/2 cups white sugar
- 1/4 teaspoon water

3 tablespoons milk

DIRECTIONS

1. Preheat oven to 350 degrees F (175 degrees C). Place rolled-out pie crust in a 9-inch pie plate and set on a baking sheet lined with parchment paper or a silicone baking mat.
2. Combine rhubarb and strawberries in a bowl; transfer to the pie crust, distributing evenly.
3. Whisk eggs, sugar, milk, flour, and nutmeg together in a medium bowl. Slowly pour filling over rhubarb mixture until it just reaches the top edge of the crust. Scatter diced butter evenly over the top of the filling. Lightly tap and shake the baking sheet to remove any air bubbles.
4. Transfer pie to the preheated oven and bake, turning halfway through, until rhubarb is tender and custard is set, about 1 hour.
5. Mix strawberry jam and water in a small bowl; heat in the microwave until warm, about 15 seconds. Glaze the top of the pie with the jam mixture and let cool. Refrigerate until ready to serve.

OLD FASHIONED PARADISE PUMPKIN PIE

Servings: 8 | Prep: 30m | Cooks: 1h | Total: 2h | Additional: 30m

NUTRITION FACTS

Calories: 430 | Carbohydrates: 40.3g | Fat: 27.1g | Protein: 8.6g | Cholesterol: 117mg**INGREDIENTS**

- 1 (9 inch) pie shell
- 1/4 cup white sugar
- 1 (8 ounce) package cream cheese, softened
- 1 teaspoon ground cinnamon
- 1/4 cup white sugar
- 1/4 teaspoon ground nutmeg
- 1/2 teaspoon vanilla extract
- 1/4 teaspoon salt
- 1 egg, beaten
- 2 tablespoons all-purpose flour
- 1 1/4 cups pumpkin puree
- 2 tablespoons brown sugar
- 1 cup evaporated milk
- 2 tablespoons butter, softened

2 eggs, beaten

DIRECTIONS

1. Preheat oven to 350 degrees F (175 degrees C).
2. To Make Cheesecake Layer: In a medium mixing bowl, beat cream cheese until smooth. Beat in 1/4 cup sugar, then add vanilla extract and 1 egg. Beat mixture until light and smooth. Chill mixture for 30 minutes, then spread into pastry shell.
3. To Make Pumpkin Layer: In a large bowl, combine pumpkin puree, evaporated milk, 2 eggs, 1/4 cup brown sugar, 1/4 cup white sugar, cinnamon, nutmeg, and salt. Mix until all ingredients are thoroughly combined.
4. Pour pumpkin mixture over cream cheese layer. Cover edges of crust with aluminum foil.
5. Bake in preheated oven for 25 minutes. Remove foil from edges and bake an additional 25 minutes.
6. To Make Pecan Streusel Layer: While pie is in oven, combine flour and 2 tablespoons brown sugar in a small bowl. Mix well, then add softened butter or margarine and stir until ingredients are combined. Mix in pecans.
7. After pie has been in oven for 50 minutes, remove and sprinkle pecan streusel evenly over top. Bake for an additional 10 to 15 minutes, until a toothpick inserted in center comes out clean.

TRUE BLUE CUSTARD CRUNCH PIE
Servings: 8 | Prep: 15m | Cooks: 40m | Total: 55m

NUTRITION FACTS

Calories: 378 | Carbohydrates: 44.3g | Fat: 21.2g | Protein: 4.3g | Cholesterol: 47mg**INGREDIENTS**

- 8 ounces sour cream
- 2 1/2 cups fresh blueberries
- 3/4 cup sugar
- 1 (9 inch) unbaked pie crust
- 1 egg
- 3 tablespoons all-purpose flour
- 2 tablespoons flour
- 2 tablespoons white sugar
- 2 teaspoons vanilla extract
- 3 tablespoons chilled butter, cut into small pieces
- 1/4 teaspoon salt

4 tablespoons chopped pecans**DIRECTIONS**

1. Preheat oven to 400 degrees F (200 degrees C).
2. Beat together sour cream, 3/4 cup sugar, egg, 2 tablespoons flour, vanilla extract and salt in a mixing bowl until smooth. Gently fold the blueberries into the sour cream mixture. Spoon the filling into the unbaked pie crust.
3. Bake in the preheated oven for 25 minutes.
4. While the filling is baking, prepare the streusel crunch topping: In a medium bowl combine 3 tablespoons flour and 2 tablespoons sugar. Cut the cold butter into the flour mixture until crumbly. Fold in the chopped pecans. After the filling has baked 25 minutes, sprinkle the streusel crunch topping over the top of the pie.
5. Bake until the topping is golden brown, about 15 additional minutes.

BANANA CREAM PIE MADE EASY
Servings: 8 | Prep: 25m | Cooks: 1h | Total: 1h25m | Additional: 1h

NUTRITION FACTS

Calories: 606 | Carbohydrates: 46.1g | Fat: 46.6g | Protein: 4.1g | Cholesterol: 143mg

INGREDIENTS

- 3 cups heavy cream
- 3 bananas, sliced
- 1/2 cup crushed ice
- 1 (9 inch) pie shell, baked
- 1 (3.5 ounce) package instant banana pudding mix
- 1 cup heavy cream

1 (3.4 ounce) package instant vanilla pudding mix

DIRECTIONS

1. Using an electric mixer, whip 3 cups heavy cream on low speed until it starts to thicken. Add crushed ice and continue to whip another 4 minutes. Increase speed and add vanilla and banana pudding mixes, whipping until pudding mixes are blended fully with the cream and the mixture thickens. Increase speed to high and beat until mixture is stiff.
2. Line the bottom and half way up the sides of pie crust with banana slices. Cover bananas with half of the banana cream mixture and top completely with banana slices. Top with the remaining banana cream mixture.
3. In a small bowl, whip 1 cup cream until stiff peaks form. Using a pastry bag, pipe cream onto top of pie, covering completely. Refrigerate 1 hour before serving.

IMPOSSIBLE PUMPKIN PIE
Servings: 8 | Prep: 25m | Cooks: 50m | Total: 1h15m

NUTRITION FACTS

Calories: 245 | Carbohydrates: 34.7g | Fat: 9.5g | Protein: 6.3g | Cholesterol: 72mg

INGREDIENTS

- 3/4 cup white sugar
- 1/2 cup all-purpose flour
- 3 tablespoons butter, softened
- 3/4 teaspoon baking powder
- 2 eggs, beaten
- 1/8 teaspoon salt
- 1 (15 ounce) can pumpkin puree
- 1 teaspoon ground cinnamon
- 1 (12 fluid ounce) can evaporated milk
- 1 teaspoon ground allspice
- 2 teaspoons vanilla extract
- 1/2 teaspoon ground ginger

1/2 teaspoon ground nutmeg

DIRECTIONS

1. Preheat oven to 350 degrees F (175 degrees C). Grease one 9-inch pie pan, and set aside.
2. Sift together the flour, baking powder, salt, cinnamon, allspice, ginger and nutmeg.
3. In a large bowl, beat together the sugar, butter and eggs. Mix in the pumpkin, milk and vanilla. Add the sifted ingredients, and beat until smooth. Pour into the prepared pan.
4. Bake at 350 degrees F (175 degrees C) for 50 to 55 minutes, or until a toothpick inserted in center comes out clean.

APPLE DELIGHT

Servings: 12 | Prep: 5m | Cooks: 30m | Total: 35m

NUTRITION FACTS

Calories: 354 | Carbohydrates: 59.6g | Fat: 12.8g | Protein: 2.1g | Cholesterol: 21mg

INGREDIENTS

- 2 (21 ounce) cans apple pie filling
- 1 (18.25 ounce) package yellow cake mix

1/2 cup butter, melted

DIRECTIONS

1. Preheat oven to 350 degrees F (175 degrees C).
2. Pour apple pie filling into a 9x13-inch pan. Sprinkle cake mix over apples. Drizzle melted butter on top, stirring slightly to evenly moisten dry cake batter. Bake 30 minutes. Serve hot or cold.

APPLE-BERRY PIE

Servings: 8 | Prep: 20m | Cooks: 50m | Total: 1h10m

NUTRITION FACTS

Calories: 385 | Carbohydrates: 54.1g | Fat: 18g | Protein: 3.4g | Cholesterol: 8mg

INGREDIENTS

- 1 pastry for a 9 inch double crust pie
- 2 cups fresh blackberries
- 1 cup white sugar
- 2 cups apples - peeled, cored and sliced
- 4 teaspoons tapioca
- 2 tablespoons butter, cut into small pieces

1/2 teaspoon ground cinnamon**DIRECTIONS**

1. Preheat oven to 375 degrees F (190 degrees C). On a lightly floured surface, roll out one crust, and place in a 9 inch pie plate. Roll out top crust, and set aside.
2. In a large bowl, mix together the sugar, tapioca, and cinnamon. Add blackberries and apple slices. Toss gently to coat without mashing the berries. Let stand for 20 minutes.
3. Spoon filling into pastry lined pan. Dot with butter. Moisten the edge of the pastry with water. Cover with top crust; trim and crimp edge. Cut a few slits in the top to allow steam to escape during baking. Cover edge with foil to prevent over-browning.

4. Bake in preheated oven for 25 minutes. Remove foil, and continue baking for 20 to 25 minutes, or until crust is golden brown. Cool on wire rack.

FRENCH APPLE TART (TARTE DE POMMES A LA NORMANDE)

Servings: 8 | Prep: 1h | Cooks: 40m | Total: 1h40m

NUTRITION FACTS

Calories: 507 | Carbohydrates: 50.1g | Fat: 32.3g | Protein: 7.3g | Cholesterol: 135mg

INGREDIENTS

- 1 1/3 cups all-purpose flour
- 1 egg yolk
- 1 pinch salt
- 1 tablespoon apple brandy
- 1/2 cup butter, softened
- 2/3 cup ground almonds
- 1 egg yolk
- 2 tablespoons all-purpose flour
- 3 tablespoons cold water, or as needed
- 4 medium sweet apples - peeled, cored, halved and thinly sliced
- 1/2 cup butter, softened
- 1 teaspoon white sugar for decoration
- 1/2 cup white sugar
- 1/4 cup apricot jelly

1 egg, beaten

DIRECTIONS

1. In a medium bowl, stir together 1 1/3 cups of flour and salt. Add the butter, 1 egg yolk and water, and stir until the mixture forms large crumbs. If it is too dry to press a handful together, stir in more water. Press the dough into a ball, and wrap in plastic wrap. Flatten slightly, and refrigerate for at least 30 minutes, or until firm. This part can be done up to three days in advance.
2. To make the frangipane, cream together the butter and 1/2 cup of sugar in a medium bowl until light and soft. Gradually mix in the egg and the remaining egg yolk one at a time. Stir in the apple brandy. Stir 2 tablespoons of flour into the ground almonds, then mix into the batter. Set aside.
3. Roll the pastry dough out to about a 12 inch circle on a lightly floured surface. Fold loosely into quarters, and center the point in a 10 inch tart or pie pan. Unfold dough, and press into the bottom and up the sides. Prick with a fork all over, and flute the edges. Return pastry to the refrigerator to chill until firm.

4. Preheat the oven to 400 degrees F (200 degrees C). Place a baking sheet inside the oven while it preheats.

5. Spoon the frangipane into the chilled pastry, and spread into an even layer. Arrange the apple slices in an overlapping spiral pattern. Each slice should have one edge pressed into the frangipane until it touches the pastry base, and then overlap the previous slice. Start at the outside edge, and work towards the center.

6. Place the pie plate on top of the baking sheet in the preheated oven. Bake for 15 minutes, or until the filling begins to brown. Reduce the oven temperature to 350 degrees F (175 degrees C). Bake for another 10 minutes, then sprinkle sugar over the top of the tart. Return to the oven for 10 more minutes, or until the sugar caramelizes slightly.

7. Cool the tart on a wire rack. A short time before serving, warm the apricot jelly. Add some water if necessary to make it a liquid consistency. Brush onto the tart for a nice shine.

LEMON PIE

Servings: 8 | Prep: 10m | Cooks: 1h | Total: 2h10m | Additional: 2h

NUTRITION FACTS

Calories: 456 | Carbohydrates: 48.2g | Fat: 27g | Protein: 7.6g | Cholesterol: 68mg

INGREDIENTS

- 1 (8 ounce) package cream cheese, room temperature
- 1 (9 inch) prepared graham cracker crust
- 1 (14 ounce) can sweetened condensed milk
- whipped cream for serving (optional)

1/3 cup lemon juice

DIRECTIONS

1. Mix together the cream cheese, milk and lemon juice. Mix well and spread in graham crust. Chill until set, at least 2 hours, and top as desired.

PIE CRUST

Servings: 16 | Prep: 20m | Cooks: 0m | Total: 20m

NUTRITION FACTS

Calories: 132 | Carbohydrates: 11.9g | Fat: 8.7g | Protein: 1.6g | Cholesterol: 0mg

INGREDIENTS

- 2 cups all-purpose flour

- 2/3 cup shortening
- 1 teaspoon salt

6 tablespoons cold water**DIRECTIONS**

1. Mix flour and salt in a large bowl. Cut in shortening with a pastry blender until mixture is completely blended and appears crumbly.
2. Mix in water, 1 tablespoon at a time, by lightly tossing with a fork. Add only enough water to form mixture into a ball. The dough will be sticky and tough if to much water is added, and it will crack and tear when rolled if too little is added.
3. Divide the dough into 2 balls, and roll each out into a circle 1 inch larger than the inverted pie plate.
4. Follow these directions for a filled pie. Fold one circle of dough in half, and gently lift. Place into pie plate and unfold. Add filling to pie plate. Fold second circle of dough in half. Gently place over filling, and unfold. With a table knife, cut off excess crust evenly so that 1/2 to 1 inch extends beyond the edge of the pie plate. Fold under the excess dough so that it is even with the edge of the pie plate. Flute the edge of the crust. Cut slits in top crust for steam to escape.
5. Follow these directions for 2 prebaked pie shells. Fold circle of dough in half, and gently lift. Place into pie plate and unfold. Either prick the entire surface of dough with a fork, or weight the bottom of the crust with pie weights while baking. Pie weights can be uncooked rice, dried beans, small clean pebbles, or small balls sold as pie weights.

PORTUGUESE CUSTARD TARTS - PASTEIS DE NATA
Servings: 12 | Prep: 20m | Cooks: 20m | Total: 40m

NUTRITION FACTS

Calories: 336 | Carbohydrates: 38.7g | Fat: 18.2g | Protein: 5g | Cholesterol: 104mg

INGREDIENTS

- 1 cup milk
- 1 cup white sugar
- 3 tablespoons cornstarch
- 6 egg yolks
- 1/2 vanilla bean
- 1 package frozen puff pastry, thawed

DIRECTIONS

1. Preheat oven to 375 degrees F (190 degrees C.) Lightly grease 12 muffin cups and line bottom and sides with puff pastry.
2. In a saucepan, combine milk, cornstarch, sugar and vanilla. Cook, stirring constantly, until mixture thickens. Place egg yolks in a medium bowl. Slowly whisk 1/2 cup of hot milk mixture into egg yolks. Gradually add egg yolk mixture back to remaining milk mixture, whisking constantly. Cook, stirring constantly, for 5 minutes, or until thickened. Remove vanilla bean.
3. Fill pastry-lined muffin cups with mixture and bake in preheated oven for 20 minutes, or until crust is golden brown and filling is lightly browned on top.

SWEDISH APPLE PIE

Servings: 8 | Prep: 15m | Cooks: 1h5m | Total: 1h20m

NUTRITION FACTS

Calories: 386 | Carbohydrates: 44.6g | Fat: 22.8g | Protein: 3.2g | Cholesterol: 17mg

INGREDIENTS

- 2 1/2 cups peeled, cored and sliced apples
- 1/2 cup chopped pecans
- 1 teaspoon ground cinnamon
- 1 cup all-purpose flour
- 1 teaspoon white sugar
- 1 egg, lightly beaten
- 1 cup white sugar
- 1 pinch salt

3/4 cup margarine, melted**DIRECTIONS**

1. Preheat oven to 350 degrees F (175 degrees C). Lightly grease a 9 inch pie pan with margarine.
2. Fill 2/3 of the pan with sliced apples. Sprinkle with cinnamon and 1 teaspoon sugar.
3. In a medium bowl, mix 1 cup sugar with the melted margarine. Stir in pecans, flour, egg and salt. Mix well. Spread mixture over the apples.
4. Bake in preheated oven for 65 minutes, or until golden brown.

MOTHER'S DAY PIE

Servings: 8 | Prep: 15m | Cooks: 35m | Total: 2h50m | Additional: 2h

NUTRITION FACTS

Calories: 314 | Carbohydrates: 36.2g | Fat: 16.7g | Protein: 6.2g | Cholesterol: 106mg**INGREDIENTS**

- 1 cup white sugar
- 1 teaspoon vanilla extract
- 2 tablespoons all-purpose flour
- 3 eggs
- 1/4 teaspoon salt
- 1 (12 fluid ounce) can evaporated milk
- 6 tablespoons butter, melted

1 cup shredded coconut **DIRECTIONS**

1. Preheat oven to 325 degrees F (165 degrees C). Generously grease and flour a 9-inch pie plate.
2. In a medium bowl, mix together sugar, flour, and salt. Stir in melted butter and vanilla extract. Add eggs one at a time, mixing well after each addition. Mix in evaporated milk followed by coconut. Pour mixture into pie plate.
3. Bake in preheated oven for 35 to 40 minutes, or until custard is nearly set and a knife inserted near the center of the pie comes out clean. Let cool, then refrigerate before serving.

VANILLA PUMPKIN PIE

Servings: 8 | Prep: 10m | Cooks: 1h | Total: 1h15m | Additional: 5m

NUTRITION FACTS

Calories: 289 | Carbohydrates: 38.4g | Fat: 12.5g | Protein: 7.1g | Cholesterol: 60mg

INGREDIENTS

- 1 1/2 cups pumpkin puree
- 1/2 teaspoon salt
- 1 (12 fluid ounce) can evaporated milk
- 1 1/4 teaspoons vanilla extract
- 2 eggs
- 1/2 teaspoon ground cinnamon
- 3/4 cup white sugar
- 1 (9 inch) unbaked pie crust

1 tablespoon all-purpose flour

DIRECTIONS

1. Preheat oven to 450 degrees F (230 degrees C).
2. In a large bowl, combine pumpkin, evaporated milk, eggs, sugar, flour, salt vanilla and cinnamon. Pour filling into pie shell.
3. Bake for 20 minutes at 450 degrees F (230 degrees C) then turn oven temperature down to 350 degrees F (175 degrees C) and continue baking 40 more minutes or until a knife inserted in center comes out clean. Cool completely on a wire rack before serving.

CHOCOLATE PEANUT BUTTER PIE

Servings: 16 | Prep: 20m | Cooks: 2h | Total: 2h20m | Additional: 2h

NUTRITION FACTS

Calories: 453 | Carbohydrates: 51.1g | Fat: 26.4g | Protein: 6.4g | Cholesterol: 25mg

INGREDIENTS

- 1 cup peanut butter
- 2 cups milk
- 3/4 cup butter
- 1 (3.9 ounce) package instant chocolate pudding mix
- 3 cups confectioners' sugar
- 1 (8 ounce) container frozen whipped topping, thawed

2 (8 inch) prepared graham cracker crusts

DIRECTIONS

1. In a medium, microwave-safe bowl, combine butter and peanut butter. Heat in the microwave until soft; mix well. Gradually stir in confectioners' sugar until the mixture resembles a soft dough. Spread mixture into 2 pie crusts.
2. In a small bowl, mix the milk with the instant pudding. Pour over the peanut butter mixture in each crust. Chill until firm.
3. Top pies with whipped topping when ready to serve.

MILK TART

Servings: 6 | Prep: 30m | Cooks: 20m | Total: 50m

NUTRITION FACTS

Calories: 241 | Carbohydrates: 35.9g | Fat: 8.8g | Protein: 5g | Cholesterol: 57mg

INGREDIENTS

- 1/2 cup butter, softened
- 1 teaspoon vanilla extract
- 1 cup white sugar
- 1 tablespoon butter
- 1 egg
- 2 1/2 tablespoons all-purpose flour
- 2 cups all-purpose flour
- 2 1/2 tablespoons cornstarch
- 2 teaspoons baking powder
- ½ cup white sugar
- 1 pinch salt
- 2 eggs, beaten
- 4 cups milk

1/2 teaspoon ground cinnamon**DIRECTIONS**

1. Preheat oven to 350 degrees F (175 degrees C).

2. In a medium mixing bowl, cream together 1/2 cup butter or margarine and 1 cup sugar. Add 1 egg and beat until mixture is smooth. In a separate bowl, mix together 2 cups flour, baking powder, and salt. Stir flour mixture into sugar mixture just until ingredients are thoroughly combined. Press mixture into bottom and sides of two 9-inch pie pans.

3. Bake in preheated oven for 10 to 15 minutes, until golden brown.

4. In a large saucepan, combine milk, vanilla extract, and 1 tablespoon butter or margarine. Bring to a boil over medium heat, then remove from burner.

5. In a separate bowl, mix together 2 1/2 tablespoons flour, cornstarch, and 1/2 cup sugar. Add beaten eggs to sugar mixture and whisk until smooth. Slowly whisk mixture into milk. Return pan to heat and bring to a boil, stirring constantly. Boil and stir 5 minutes. Pour half of mixture into each pastry shell. Sprinkle with cinnamon. Chill before serving.

TWO TIER STRAWBERRY PIE

Servings: 8 | Prep: 20m | Cooks: 10m | Total: 1h30m | Additional: 1h

NUTRITION FACTS

Calories: 378 | Carbohydrates: 41.6g | Fat: 22.6g | Protein: 3.1g | Cholesterol: 52mg

INGREDIENTS

- 1 (3 ounce) package cream cheese
- 1/3 cup white sugar
- 1/2 cup confectioners' sugar
- 2 tablespoons cornstarch
- 1/2 teaspoon vanilla extract
- 1/3 cup water
- 1/2 teaspoon almond extract
- 1/3 cup grenadine syrup
- 1 cup heavy cream
- 1 tablespoon lemon juice
- 1 (9 inch) baked pie shell

2 cups fresh strawberries, hulled**DIRECTIONS**

1. In a medium bowl, mix together cream cheese and confectioners' sugar until smooth and creamy. Stir in vanilla and almond extract. In a separate bowl, whip cream until peaks form. Fold into cream cheese mixture. Spread over bottom of baked pie shell. Chill.

2. In a saucepan, mix together sugar and cornstarch. Stir in water until smooth. Add grenadine and lemon juice. Bring to a boil over medium heat. Cook 5 minutes, stirring constantly, or until thickened. Allow to cool, then chill.

3. Just before serving, stir together strawberries and cooled cornstarch mixture until evenly coated. Spread over cream cheese layer.

RENEE'S STRAWBERRY RHUBARB PIE

Servings: 8 | Prep: 30m | Cooks: 55m | Total: 4h25m | Additional: 3h

NUTRITION FACTS

Calories: 391 | Carbohydrates: 61.1g | Fat: 15.2g | Protein: 3.9g | Cholesterol: 0mg

INGREDIENTS

- 2 tablespoons cornstarch
- 3/4 teaspoon ground cinnamon
- 1 tablespoon water
- 1 teaspoon vanilla extract
- 2 1/2 cups diced rhubarb
- 1 recipe pastry for a 9 inch double crust pie
- 2 1/2 cups sliced fresh strawberries
- 1 egg white
- 1 1/4 cups white sugar
- 1 teaspoon water
- 1/2teaspoon lemon juice

1 tablespoon turbinado sugar (such as Sugar in the Raw) **DIRECTIONS**

1. In a bowl, whisk together the cornstarch with 1 tablespoon of water until thoroughly combined. Stir in the rhubarb, strawberries, white sugar, lemon juice, cinnamon, and vanilla extract. Allow the mixture to stand for 30 minutes.
2. Preheat oven to 425 degrees F (220 degrees C). Place bottom crust into a 9-inch pie dish. Roll the remaining crust out into a 10-inch circle on a floured work surface, and set aside.
3. Stir the filling, and pour into the prepared pie dish. Cut the remaining crust into 1-inch wide strips (use a scalloped edge pastry cutter for a prettier crust). Moisten the rim of the filled bottom crust with a bit of water, and lay the two longest strips in a cross in the middle of the pie. Working from the next longest down to the shortest strips, alternate horizontal and vertical strips, weaving the strips as you go. Press the lattice strips down onto the bottom crust edge to seal, and trim the top crust strips neatly. Beat the egg white with 1 teaspoon of water in a small bowl, and brush the entire lattice top with the beaten egg white. Sprinkle with turbinado sugar. Wrap aluminum foil strips around the edges of the pie.
4. Bake in the preheated oven for 15 minutes; reduce heat to 375 degrees F (190 degrees C), and bake until the crust is browned and the filling is bubbling, 40 to 45 more minutes. Remove the aluminum foil for the last 10 minutes of baking time. Allow pie to cool completely before serving.

PUMPKIN PIE SPICE

Servings: 8 | Prep: 1m | Cooks: 0m | Total: 1m

NUTRITION FACTS

Calories: 21 | Carbohydrates: 4.7g | Fat: 0.7g | Protein: 0.4g | Cholesterol: 0mg

INGREDIENTS

- 1/4 cup ground cinnamon
- 4 teaspoons ground nutmeg
- 4 teaspoons ground ginger

1 tablespoon ground allspice**DIRECTIONS**

1. Combine cinnamon, nutmeg, ginger, and allspice together in a bowl. Store in air-tight container.

CHOCOLATE LAYERED PIE

Servings: 8 | Prep: 20m | Cooks: 10m | Total: 2h30m | Additional: 2h

NUTRITION FACTS

Calories: 542 | Carbohydrates: 54.8g | Fat: 34.3g | Protein: 6g | Cholesterol: 63mg

INGREDIENTS

- 1/2 cup chopped pecans
- 1 cup confectioners' sugar
- 1/2 cup butter, melted
- 1 (5.9 ounce) package instant chocolate pudding mix
- 1 cup all-purpose flour
- 2/3 cup milk
- 1 cup frozen whipped topping, thawed
- 2 cups frozen whipped topping, thawed

1 (8 ounce) package cream cheese

DIRECTIONS

1. Mix together pecans, melted butter, and flour. Pat into the bottom and up the sides of a 9 inch pie plate. Bake at 350 degrees F (175 degrees C) until lightly browned. Remove from oven, and set aside to cool.
2. In a mixing bowl, blend 1 cup whipped topping, cream cheese, and confectioners sugar until creamy. Spread into cooled crust.
3. Whisk together pudding mix and milk. Spread evenly over cheese layer, and the spread remaining whipped topping on top. Chill 1 1/2 to 2 hours.

MARGARET'S SOUTHERN CHOCOLATE PIE

Servings: 8 | Prep: 35m | Cooks: 25m | Total: 1h

NUTRITION FACTS

Calories: 432 | Carbohydrates: 62.9g | Fat: 17.7g | Protein: 8g | Cholesterol: 102mg

INGREDIENTS

- 1/4 cup unsweetened cocoa powder
- 3 tablespoons butter
- 1/4 cup all-purpose flour
- 1 (9 inch) pie shell, baked
- 3 egg yolks
- 3 egg whites
- 1 1/3 cups white sugar
- 1/8 teaspoon cream of tartar
- 1 (12 fluid ounce) can evaporated milk

6 tablespoons white sugar **DIRECTIONS**

1. Preheat oven to 350 degrees F (175 degrees C).
2. Sift together the cocoa powder and the flour and pour them into a saucepan. Whisk the egg yolks and 1 1/3 cups sugar. Gradually add the evaporated milk, whisking constantly; slowly pour the milk mixture into the saucepan, whisking until combined.
3. Cook over medium heat, stirring constantly with a flat-bottomed wooden spoon or spatula, until the mixture begins to thicken and coats the back of the spoon, about 15 minutes. Remove the custard from the heat and stir in the butter until melted. Pour the filling into the baked pie crust.
4. To make the meringue topping: Combine the egg whites and cream of tartar in a clean glass or metal bowl; beat with an electric mixer until foamy. Gradually add sugar, a tablespoon at a time, continuing to beat until stiff peaks form. Lift your beater or whisk straight up: the egg whites will form sharp peaks. Spread the meringue over the chocolate filling.
5. Bake in the preheated oven for 10 minutes, or until the tips of the meringue peaks are golden brown.

GRAHAM CRACKER CRUST

Servings: 8 | Prep: 5m | Cooks: 8m | Total: 14m

NUTRITION FACTS

Calories: 110 | Carbohydrates: 10.8g | Fat: 7.2g | Protein: 1g | Cholesterol: 15mg

INGREDIENTS

- 16 graham cracker squares, crushed

1/4 cup butter, melted**DIRECTIONS**

1. Preheat oven to 350 degrees F (175 degrees C).
2. In a medium bowl, mix together graham cracker crumbs and melted margarine. Place mixture in a 9 inch pie pan and press firmly into bottom and sides of pan.
3. Bake in preheated oven for 8 minutes.

APPLE HAND PIES

Servings: 4 | Prep: 25m | Cooks: 35m | Total: 1h15m | Additional: 15m

NUTRITION FACTS

Calories: 729 | Carbohydrates: 82.3g | Fat: 42g | Protein: 8.5g | Cholesterol: 62mg

INGREDIENTS

- 1 pound prepared pie dough, cut into 4 pieces
- 1 1/2 teaspoons ground cinnamon, or to taste
- 2 large green apples, peeled and cored
- 1 teaspoon water, or more if needed (optional)
- 2 tablespoons butter
- 1 egg
- 1/4 teaspoon salt
- 2 teaspoons milk
- 1/4 cup white sugar
- 1 teaspoon white sugar, or as needed - divided

2 tablespoons brown sugar

DIRECTIONS

1. Line a baking sheet with a silicone mat or parchment paper.
2. Cut peeled and cored apples into quarters, cut each quarter into 3 wedges, and cut wedges into chunks.
3. Melt butter in a large skillet over medium heat; let butter brown to a light golden color and until butter smells toasted, about 1 minute. Stir apples into hot butter; sprinkle with salt, white sugar, and brown sugar. Cook and stir apple mixture until apples are softened, about 5 minutes. Mix in cinnamon and water; continue cooking until apples are soft and sticky, 1 to 2 more minutes. Spread apple filling onto a plate to cool.
4. Preheat oven to 400 degrees F (200 degrees C).
5. Form a dough piece into a ball, place on a floured work surface, and roll into a circle about 8 inches in diameter. Spoon 1/3 to 1/2 cup apple filling in the center. Fold dough over filling, leaving about 1 inch of dough on the bottom side visible below the top side. Gently press dough closed around filling, using your fingertips.

6. Fold the overhanging bottom part of the dough up over the top edge, working your way around the crust, and pinch the overhang tightly to the top part of the crust.
7. Crimp the edge tightly closed, pinching a little bit of dough with the thumb and forefinger of one hand and using your index finger on the other hand to push a small notch into the pinched dough. Continue pinching and notching all the way around until the crust is tightly crimped together. Repeat with remaining dough and filling. Transfer pies onto prepared baking sheet.
8. Whisk egg with milk in a small bowl until thoroughly combined. Brush top of each hand pie with egg mixture and sprinkle with about 1/4 teaspoon white sugar. Cut 3 small vent holes in the top of each pie.
9. Bake in the preheated oven until pies are golden brown and filling is bubbling, 25 to 30 minutes. Let cool for at least 15 minutes before serving.

BUTTERMILK PIE
Servings: 8 | Prep: 10m | Cooks: 1hm | Total: 1h15m | Additional: 5m

NUTRITION FACTS

Calories: 405 | Carbohydrates: 50.2g | Fat: 21.2g | Protein: 5g | Cholesterol: 101mg**INGREDIENTS**

- 1/2 cup butter
- 1 cup buttermilk
- 1 1/2 cups white sugar
- 1 teaspoon vanilla extract
- 3 teaspoons all-purpose flour
- 1/4 teaspoon ground nutmeg
- 3 eggs

1 (9 inch) unbaked pie crust **DIRECTIONS**

1. Preheat oven to 350 degrees F (175 degrees C).
2. In a large bowl, cream butter and sugar until smooth. mix in the flour, eggs, buttermilk and vanilla. Pour filling into pie shell. Sprinkle top with nutmeg.
3. Bake in the preheated oven for 60 minutes, or until golden brown.

APPLE SLAB PIE
Servings: 15 | Prep: 30m | Cooks: 1h | Total: 1h30m

NUTRITION FACTS

Calories: 405 | Carbohydrates: 61.5g | Fat: 17.5g | Protein: 2.9g | Cholesterol: 53mg

INGREDIENTS

- 1 1/2 cups all-purpose flour
- 2 tablespoons all-purpose flour
- 1 1/2 tablespoons white sugar
- 1 3/4 cups white sugar
- 1/2 cup shortening
- 1/2 teaspoon ground cinnamon
- 1/4 teaspoon salt
- 2 tablespoons butter
- 1/2 teaspoon baking powder
- 1 cup all-purpose flour
- 2 egg yolks, beaten
- 1 teaspoon ground cinnamon
- 4 tablespoons water
- 2/3 cup brown sugar
- 8 apples - peeled, cored and cut into thin wedges
- 2/3 cup butter

2 tablespoons lemon juice

DIRECTIONS

1. Preheat oven to 350 degrees F (175 degrees C.) In a large bowl, combine flour sugar, salt and baking powder. Cut in shortening until mixture resembles coarse crumbs. Mix egg yolk and water together and mix into flour until it forms a ball. Roll out to fit the bottom of a 10x15 inch pan.
2. In a large bowl, combine apples, lemon juice, 2 tablespoons flour, sugar and cinnamon. Pour filling into pie crust and dot with 2 tablespoons butter.
3. In a medium bowl, combine 1 cup flour, 1 teaspoon cinnamon, 2/3 cup brown sugar and 2/3 cup butter. Cut in the butter until crumbly, then sprinkle over apples.
4. Bake in the preheated oven for 60 minutes, or until topping is golden brown.

EMILY'S FAMOUS APPLE PIE

Servings: 10 | Prep: 15m | Cooks: 45m | Total: 1h

NUTRITION FACTS

Calories: 299 | Carbohydrates: 47.2g | Fat: 12g | Protein: 3g | Cholesterol: 0mg

INGREDIENTS

- 2/3 cup white sugar
- 1/4 teaspoon ground cloves
- 1/3 cup all-purpose flour
- 1 recipe pastry for a 9 inch double crust pie

- 1 tablespoon ground cinnamon

8 Granny Smith apple - peeled, cored and sliced **DIRECTIONS**

1. Preheat oven to 350 degrees F (175 degrees C).
2. In a small bowl stir together the sugar, flour, cinnamon and cloves.
3. Place one of the pie shells into a 10 inch pie pan. Put 1/2 of the sliced apples into the shell and sprinkle half of the sugar mixture over them. Top with the remaining apples and the remaining sugar mixture.
4. Cover apples with the top crust. Press edges with the tines of a fork to seal and poke holes in the top with a knife. Bake in preheated oven for 45 minutes.

OCTOBER APPLE PIE
Servings: 8 | Prep: 30m | Cooks: 50m | Total: 1h20m

NUTRITION FACTS

Calories: 379 | Carbohydrates: 63.7g | Fat: 14.4g | Protein: 2.7g | Cholesterol: 16mg

INGREDIENTS

- 1 recipe pastry for a 9 inch double crust pie
- 1/4 teaspoon freshly grated nutmeg
- 6 cups thinly sliced apples
- 3 tablespoons all-purpose flour
- 1 lemon, juiced
- 1/4 cup butter, chilled and diced
- 1/2 cup packed light brown sugar
- 9 caramel squares, quartered
- 1/2 cup white sugar
- 1 tablespoon white sugar

2 teaspoons ground cinnamon

DIRECTIONS

1. In a large bowl, combine apples, lemon juice, sugars, spices, flour, butter, and caramels. Stir to coat fruit evenly.
2. Roll dough out, and cut out two crusts. Line a pie plate with one of the crusts. Spoon filling into the bottom crust, and cover with the top crust. Crimp the edges. Place the pie on a baking sheet covered with foil. Poke fork holes over top. Sprinkle lightly with granulated sugar.
3. Bake at 375 degrees F (190 degrees C) for 50 minutes. If you notice overbrowning after 30 minutes, reduce heat to 350 degrees F (175 degrees C). Serve warm, or at room temperature.

TOASTED COCONUT, PECAN, AND CARAMEL PIE

Servings: 16 | Prep: 30m | Cooks: 10m | Total: 1h40m | Additional: 1h

NUTRITION FACTS

Calories: 479 | Carbohydrates: 50.9g | Fat: 29.4g | Protein: 5.8g | Cholesterol: 32mg

INGREDIENTS

- 2 (9 inch) pie shells, baked
- 1 (8 ounce) package cream cheese, softened
- 1/4 cup butter
- 1 (14 ounce) can sweetened condensed milk
- 1 (8 ounce) package flaked coconut
- 1 (12 ounce) container frozen whipped topping, thawed
- 1/2 cup chopped pecans

1 (12 ounce) jar caramel ice cream topping **DIRECTIONS**

1. In a medium skillet, melt butter or margarine over medium heat. Add coconut and pecans. Toss well, and saute until coconut is lightly browned. Set aside to cool.
2. In a large mixing bowl, beat cream cheese until fluffy. Add condensed milk and mix until smooth. Fold in whipped topping. Spread 1/4 of cream cheese mixture into each pastry shell. Sprinkle 1/4 of coconut mixture over each pie. Drizzle 1/2 of caramel topping over each coconut layer. Follow with remaining cream cheese mixture, then remaining coconut mixture.
3. Pies may be served chilled or frozen.

APPLE CRUNCH PIE

Servings: 8 | Prep: 30m | Cooks: 1h | Total: 1h30m

NUTRITION FACTS

Calories: 490 | Carbohydrates: 79.6g | Fat: 19.2g | Protein: 3.4g | Cholesterol: 31mg

INGREDIENTS

- 1 (9 inch) unbaked deep dish pie crust
- 7 Granny Smith apples - peeled, cored and sliced
- 1 cup all-purpose flour
- 1 tablespoon lemon juice
- 1/2 cup packed brown sugar
- 1/2 cup white sugar
- 1/2 cup white sugar
- 3 tablespoons all-purpose flour

- 1 teaspoon ground cinnamon
- 1 teaspoon ground cinnamon
- 1/2 cup butter

1/8 teaspoon ground nutmeg **DIRECTIONS**

1. Place rack in lowest position in oven. Heat oven to 450 degrees F (230 degrees C).
2. To Make Topping: Mix 1 cup flour, 1/2 cup brown sugar, 1/2 cup white sugar and 1 teaspoon cinnamon; cut in butter or margarine until mixture is moist and crumbly, and clumps together easily.
3. To Make Filling: Peel, core, and slice apples into approximately 1/8 inch slices. If you cut them too thick you'll have crunchy apples. In another bowl, toss cut up apples, white sugar, lemon juice, 1 teaspoon cinnamon and nutmeg. Sprinkle in flour, and stir until apples are evenly coated.
4. Layer apple slices in pie shell. You will have a lot of apples, but they will shrink. Layer them higher in the middle. Pour left over juice from apple mixture over apples. Pat the brown sugar topping evenly over apples to make a top crust.
5. Place pie on cookie sheet in oven to catch juice droppings. Bake for 15 minutes. Reduce oven temperature to 350 degrees F (175 degrees C), and bake for 45 minutes to one hour; bake until center of pie has no resistance. If top starts to get too dark, cover with piece of foil. Cool on wire rack before serving.

SOUR CREAM LEMON PIE

Servings: 8 | Prep: 30m | Cooks: 1h30m | Total: 11h | Additional: 9h

NUTRITION FACTS

Calories: 340 | Carbohydrates: 43.2g | Fat: 16.9g | Protein: 5g | Cholesterol: 103mg

INGREDIENTS

- 1 cup white sugar
- 3 egg yolks
- 1/2 cup all-purpose flour
- 1/4 cup butter
- 1/2 teaspoon salt
- 1 1/2 teaspoons lemon zest
- 2 cups milk
- 1/4 cup lemon juice
- 1/2 cup sour cream

1 (9 inch) pie crust, baked **DIRECTIONS**

1. In a saucepan, combine sugar, flour, and salt. Gradually stir in milk. Cook and stir on medium heat until thickened and bubbly. Reduce heat, and cook and stir 2 more minutes. Remove from heat.

2. Beat yolks slightly. Gradually stir 1 cup of mix into yolks. Return yolk mixture to saucepan, and bring to gentle boil. Cook and stir 2 more minutes. Remove from heat, and stir in butter, peel, and juice. Fold in sour cream.
3. Pour filling into baked pie shell, and cool. Top with whipped cream if desired.

SINGLE CRUST PEACH PIE

Servings: 8 | Prep: 30m | Cooks: 1h | Total: 1h20m | Additional: 50m

NUTRITION FACTS8

Calories: 250 | Carbohydrates: 37.5g | Fat: 10.4g | Protein: 2g | Cholesterol: mg

INGREDIENTS

- 3/4 cup white sugar
- 1/4 teaspoon ground nutmeg
- 2 tablespoons butter, softened
- 6 fresh peaches - pitted, skinned, and sliced
- 1/3 cup all-purpose flour

1 recipe pastry for a 9 inch single crust pie **DIRECTIONS**

1. Cream sugar and butter or margarine together. Add flour and nutmeg; mix until mealy. Spread 1/2 of mixture in pie crust. Arrange peaches on top of crumb mixture. Sprinkle remaining crumb mixture on top of peaches.
2. Bake at 450 degrees F (230 degrees C) for ten minutes. Reduce heat to 350 degrees F (175 degrees C). Continue baking for 40 minutes, or until brown.

NO FAIL BEAN PIE

Servings: 12 | Prep: 30m | Cooks: 50m | Total: 2h20m | Additional: 1h

NUTRITION FACTS

Calories: 539 | Carbohydrates: 75.2g | Fat: 22g | Protein: 11.2g | Cholesterol: 95mg

INGREDIENTS

- 2 deep-dish prepared pie crusts (optional)
- 2 tablespoons all-purpose flour
- 2 (15.5 ounce) cans navy beans, rinsed and drained
- 2 1/2 cups white sugar
- 1 (12 fluid ounce) can evaporated milk
- 2 tablespoons vanilla extract
- 1/2 cup butter, melted

- 2 eggs
- 1 teaspoon ground cinnamon
- 2 egg yolks

1 teaspoon grated nutmeg

DIRECTIONS

1. Preheat oven to 450 degrees F (230 degrees C). Place pie crusts into 9-inch pie dishes.
2. In a food processor, place the navy beans, evaporated milk, melted butter, cinnamon, nutmeg, flour, sugar, vanilla extract, eggs, and egg yolks; pulse the mixture a few times, then process until smooth, about 1 minute. Pour the filling into the prepared pie crusts.
3. Bake at 450 degrees F (230 degrees C) for 15 minutes, then reduce heat to 350 degrees F (175 degrees C) and bake until the filling is set and the crust is golden brown, an additional 35 minutes. Cool before slicing. Eat warm or cold. Refrigerate leftovers.

CHERRY CREAM CHEESE PIE
Servings: 8 | Prep: 15m | Cooks: 4h35m | Total: 4h45m | Additional: 4h30m

NUTRITION FACTS

Calories: 492 | Carbohydrates: 68.7g | Fat: 21.5g | Protein: 7.6g | Cholesterol: 47mg

INGREDIENTS

- 1 (9 inch) prepared graham cracker crust
- 1 (14 ounce) can sweetened condensed milk
- 1 (21 ounce) can light cherry pie filling
- 1/3 cup lemon juice
- 1 (8 ounce) package cream cheese, softened

1 teaspoon vanilla extract **DIRECTIONS**

1. Beat cream cheese until light and fluffy. Gradually add sweetened condensed milk, and continue beating until smooth and combined. Add lemon juice and vanilla; mix well.
2. Fill graham cracker crust evenly. Refrigerate until set; this will take between 2 to 4 hours. Just before serving, spread the cherry pie filling over the top of the pie.

HOME MADE TOP TARTS
Servings: 8 | Prep: 20m | Cooks: 10m | Total: 50m | Additional: 20m

NUTRITION FACTS

Calories: 398 | Carbohydrates: 60.8g | Fat: 16.3g | Protein: 3.1g | Cholesterol: 0mg

INGREDIENTS

- 1 (15 ounce) package refrigerated pie crusts
- 1/2 teaspoon vanilla extract
- 1/4 cup strawberry jam, divided
- 1 tablespoon colored decorating sugar, or as needed

2 cups confectioners' sugar

DIRECTIONS

1. Preheat oven to 425 degrees F (220 degrees C). Line baking sheets with parchment paper.
2. Unroll the pie crusts, place on a lightly floured work surface, and roll the crusts slightly with a rolling pin to square the edges. Cut each crust into 8 equal-sized rectangles. Place about 2 teaspoons of strawberry jam in the center of 8 squares, and spread the jam out to within 1/4 inch of the edge of the pastry square. Top each with another pastry square, and use a fork to crimp the squares together, sealing in the jam. Use a knife to trim the pastries, if desired. Move the filled pastries to the prepared baking sheets.
3. Bake in the preheated oven until the edges are lightly golden brown, about 7 minutes. Allow to cool on the baking sheets. Meanwhile, stir together the confectioners' sugar, milk, and vanilla extract in a bowl to make a spreadable frosting. Spread the cooled tarts with frosting and sprinkle with colored sugar.

GRANDMA'S BUTTERSCOTCH PIE

Servings: 8 | Prep: 25m | Cooks: 35m | Total: 1h

NUTRITION FACTS

Calories: 259 | Carbohydrates: 41.5g | Fat: 8.9g | Protein: 3.4g | Cholesterol: 60mg

INGREDIENTS

- 1 cup packed light brown sugar
- 2 egg yolks, beaten
- 4 tablespoons cornstarch
- 1 tablespoon butter
- 1/2 teaspoon salt
- 1 teaspoon vanilla extract
- 2 cups milk

1 (9 inch) pie crust, baked **DIRECTIONS**

1. In top of double boiler, combine brown sugar, cornstarch, salt and milk. Cook, stirring constantly, until mixture starts to thicken, about 20 minutes.
2. Whisk in egg yolks; continue to cook and stir until filling is thickened.

3. While pudding mixture is cooking, preheat the oven to 400 degrees F (200 degrees C).
4. Remove filling from heat, and stir in butter and vanilla.

Pour filling into prepared pie crust. Bake in preheated oven until top begins to brown, about 5 minutes.

TAR HEEL PIE

Servings: 12 | Prep: 20m | Cooks: 40m | Total: 1h

NUTRITION FACTS

Calories: 394 | Carbohydrates: 40.7g | Fat: 25.7g | Protein: 3.9g | Cholesterol: 51mg

INGREDIENTS

- 1/2 cup butter, melted
- 1 teaspoon vanilla extract
- 3/4 cup chocolate chips
- 1 cup chopped pecans
- 1/2 cup all-purpose flour
- 1/2 cup flaked coconut
- 1/2 cup brown sugar
- 1/4 cup chocolate chips
- 1/2 cup white sugar
- 1 (9 inch) deep dish pie crust

2 eggs, beaten

DIRECTIONS

1. Preheat oven to 350 degrees F (175 degrees C.)
2. In a large bowl, pour warm melted butter over 3/4 cup chocolate chips. Stir until smooth. Mix together flour, brown sugar, and white sugar, then stir into chocolate mixture. Stir in eggs and vanilla. Fold in pecans, coconut, and 1/4 cup chocolate chips. Pour into pie crust.
3. Bake in preheated oven for 35 to 40 minutes. Top should be set, and may crack slightly, but the pie is best if under-baked.

THE BEST LEMON TART EVER

Servings: 8 | Prep: 15m | Cooks: 35m | Total: 1h20m | Additional: 30m

NUTRITION FACTS

Calories: 507 | Carbohydrates: 78.8g | Fat: 19.5g | Protein: 6.2g | Cholesterol: 116mg

INGREDIENTS

- 3/4 cup butter, at room temperature
- 3 large eggs
- 1/2 cup white sugar
- 1 tablespoon lemon zest
- 1/2 teaspoon vanilla extract
- 1/2 cup freshly squeezed lemon juice
- 1 pinch salt
- 1/2 cup all-purpose flour
- 1 3/4 cups all-purpose flour
- 1 teaspoon confectioners' sugar, or to taste

1 1/2 cups white sugar

DIRECTIONS

1. Combine butter, 1/2 cup sugar, vanilla extract, and salt in the mixing bowl of a stand mixer; mix ingredients thoroughly with a paddle attachment. Mix flour into butter mixture to make a smooth dough. Press dough into a 9-inch tart pan; refrigerate crust for 30 minutes.
2. Preheat oven to 350 degrees F (175 degrees C).
3. Bake crust until light golden brown, 15 to 20 minutes.
4. Whisk sugar, eggs, lemon zest, lemon juice, and 1/2 cup flour in a bowl until smooth. Pour lemon filling into crust. Cover edges of crust with strips of aluminum foil to prevent burning.
5. Bake tart until filling is set, about 20 minutes. Cool completely and dust with confectioners' sugar.

CREAMY CHOCOLATE MOUSSE PIE

Servings: 10 | Prep: 20m | Cooks: 10m | Total: 3h30m | Additional: 3h

NUTRITION FACTS

Calories: 399 | Carbohydrates: 29.1g | Fat: 30.5g | Protein: 3.5g | Cholesterol: 71mg

INGREDIENTS

- 1 1/2 cups miniature marshmallows
- 2 cups heavy whipping cream
- 1 (7 ounce) bar milk chocolate candy
- 1 (9 inch) pie shell, baked

1/2 cup milk

DIRECTIONS

1. Heat marshmallows, chocolate candy, and milk in a saucepan over low heat until marshmallows and chocolate are melted, stirring constantly. Allow mixture to cool completely.

2. Beat heavy cream in a large bowl until until stiff peaks form. Lift your beater or whisk straight up: the whipped cream will form sharp peaks. Gently fold cooled chocolate mixture in whipped cream until well mixed; pour into baked pie shell. Refrigerate until set, about 3 hours.

FRENCH COCONUT PIE
Servings: 12 | Prep: 10m | Cooks: 45m | Total: 55m

NUTRITION FACTS

Calories: 438 | Carbohydrates: 52.5g | Fat: 23.9g | Protein: 5.8g | Cholesterol: 94mg

INGREDIENTS

- 2 1/4 cups white sugar
- 1/2 cup margarine, melted
- 2 tablespoons all-purpose flour
- 1 cup flaked coconut
- 6 eggs
- 1 cup chopped pecans
- 1 cup buttermilk

2 prepared 8 inch pastry shells **DIRECTIONS**

1. Preheat oven to 350 degrees F (175 degrees C). In a small bowl, mix together the sugar and flour.
2. In a large bowl, mix the eggs with a wire whisk. Whisk flour mixture into eggs, until smooth. Stir in buttermilk, margarine, coconut and pecans. Pour into unbaked pie crusts.
3. Bake in preheated oven for 45 minutes. If making a 9 inch deep dish pie, bake for 1 hour.

ENGLISH BUTTER TARTS
Servings: 12 | Prep: 20m | Cooks: 15m | Total: 35m

NUTRITION FACTS

Calories: 270 | Carbohydrates: 41.9g | Fat: 11g | Protein: 2.6g | Cholesterol: 16mg

INGREDIENTS

- 12 (2 inch) unbaked tart shells
- 1 egg
- 1/2 cup packed brown sugar
- 1 teaspoon vanilla extract
- 1/2 cup light corn syrup
- 1/4 teaspoon salt

- 1/4 cup shortening

3/4 cup raisins

DIRECTIONS

1. Preheat oven to 400 degrees F (200 degrees C).
2. Arrange tart shells on a baking sheet. Distribute raisins evenly into shells. In a large bowl, combine brown sugar, corn syrup, shortening, egg, vanilla and salt. Mix until smooth, and pour over raisins in shells.
3. Bake in preheated oven for 12 to 15 minutes or until done. Be careful not to over bake.

AMERICAN PUMPKIN PIE
Servings: 8 | Prep: 10m | Cooks: 40m | Total: 50m

NUTRITION FACTS

Calories: 287 | Carbohydrates: 41g | Fat: 11.7g | Protein: 5.8g | Cholesterol: 37mg

INGREDIENTS

- 1 egg
- 1/2 teaspoon ground cinnamon
- 1 tablespoon all-purpose flour
- 1/2 teaspoon ground ginger
- 3/4 cup white sugar
- 1/4 teaspoon ground nutmeg
- 1/2 teaspoon salt
- 2 tablespoons light corn syrup
- 1 1/2 cups pumpkin puree
- 1 (9 inch) unbaked pie crust

1 1/2 cups evaporated milk

DIRECTIONS

1. Preheat oven to 450 degrees F (230 degrees C).
2. Add the sugar gradually to the pumpkin puree. Beat well an stir in the flour, salt and spices. Stir in the corn syrup and beat well. Stir in the slightly beaten egg, then slowly add the evaporated milk, mixing until well blended. Pour the batter into the unbaked pie shell.

Bake at 450 degrees F (230 degrees C) for 10 minutes then reduce the oven temperature to 325 degrees F (165 degrees F) and continue baking pie for an additional 30 minutes or until a knife inserted into the mixture comes out clean. MULBERRY PIE

Servings: 8 | Prep: 45m | Cooks: 45m | Total: 1h30m

NUTRITION FACTS

Calories: 433 | Carbohydrates: 63.5g | Fat: 19.1g | Protein: 3.4g | Cholesterol: 8mg

INGREDIENTS

- 3 cups mulberries
- 1 recipe pastry for a 9 inch double crust pie
- 1 1/4 cups white sugar
- 2 tablespoons butter
- 1/4 cup all-purpose flour

1 tablespoon milk **DIRECTIONS**

1. Preheat oven to 400 degrees F (200 degrees C).
2. In a large bowl, mix berries with sugar and flour. Place mixture into bottom pie crust. Dot with butter and then cover with top pie crust. Crimp edges, cut slits in upper crust, and brush with milk. Let pie rest in refrigerator for 30 minutes.
3. Bake pie in preheated oven for 15 minutes. Lower oven temperature to 350 degrees F (175 degrees C) and bake for an additional 30 minutes. Remove pie from oven and let sit on wire rack until cool.

KEY LIME PIE

Servings: 8 | Prep: 20m | Cooks: 15m | Total: 1h35m | Additional: 1h

NUTRITION FACTS

Calories: 345 | Carbohydrates: 51.7g | Fat: 12.8g | Protein: 7.3g | Cholesterol: 87mg

INGREDIENTS

- 1 (14 ounce) can sweetened condensed milk
- 1 egg
- 1/2 cup key lime juice
- 1 (9 inch) prepared graham cracker crust
- 1 teaspoon grated lime zest
- 2 egg whites
- 2 egg yolks

4 tablespoons white sugar

DIRECTIONS

1. In a medium bowl, blend together condensed milk, lime juice and zest. Mix in egg yolks and whole egg. Pour mixture into crust, then cover and refrigerate for 1 hour.
2. Preheat oven to 350 degrees F (175 degrees C).
3. To Make Meringue: In a large glass or metal mixing bowl, beat egg whites until foamy. Gradually add sugar, continuing to beat until whites form stiff peaks. Spread meringue over pie, covering completely.
4. Bake in preheated oven for 15 minutes. Chill before serving.

CLASSIC KEY LIME PIE
Servings: 8 | Prep: 30m | Cooks: 10m | Total: 1h40m

NUTRITION FACTS

Calories: 731 | Carbohydrates: 51.6g | Fat: g | Protein: 6.1g | Cholesterol: 99mg

INGREDIENTS

- 1 1/4 cups graham cracker crumbs
- 2 teaspoons grated lime peel
- 2 tablespoons sugar
- Topping:
- 5 tablespoons butter, melted
- 1 cup heavy whipping cream
- 2 (14 ounce) cans EAGLE BRAND Sweetened Condensed Milk
- 1/4 cup powdered sugar
- 2/3 cup fresh lime juice
- 1/2 teaspoon vanilla extract

1/3 cup sour cream

DIRECTIONS

1. Heat oven to 325 degrees F. Combine graham cracker crumbs and sugar. Add melted butter and stir until evenly moistened. Press mixture into bottom and sides of a 9-inch pie plate to form crust. Bake 10 minutes or until crust begins to brown. Cool 15 minutes on wire rack.
2. Whisk sweetened condensed milk, lime juice and sour cream in large bowl until blended. Stir in lime peel. Pour filling into crust. Bake 7 to 10 minutes or until tiny bubbles begin to form on surface of pie. Cool completely on wire rack.
3. Beat cream, powdered sugar and vanilla in large mixing bowl with electric mixer on medium speed until stiff. Top pie with whipped cream. Chill at least 1 hour before serving. Best served the same day.

KILLER PUMPKIN PIE

Servings: 8 | Prep: 20m | Cooks: 1h | Total: 1h20m

NUTRITION FACTS

Calories: 390 | Carbohydrates: 49.6g | Fat: 19.6g | Protein: 5.4g | Cholesterol: 47mg

INGREDIENTS

- 1 1/2 cups all-purpose flour plus
- 1/2 teaspoon salt
- 2 tablespoons all-purpose flour
- 1/2 teaspoon ground ginger
- 2 teaspoons white sugar
- 1/4 teaspoon ground nutmeg
- 1 teaspoon salt
- 1/4 teaspoon ground cloves
- 1/2 cup canola oil
- 1 (15 ounce) can pumpkin puree
- 2 tablespoons rice milk
- 2 tablespoons canola oil
- 1/2 cup white sugar
- 2 large eggs
- 1/4 cup dark brown sugar
- 1 teaspoon vanilla
- 2 teaspoons ground cinnamon

1 1/4 cups rice milk **DIRECTIONS**

1. Preheat an oven to 425 degrees F (220 degrees C).
2. Stir together the flour, sugar, and salt in a 9 inch pie pan, and make a well in the center. Pour the oil and rice milk into the well, then mix with a fork until a dough forms. Use your hands to press the mixture evenly into the bottom and sides of the pan. Crimp the edge of the crust.
3. Stir together the white sugar, brown sugar, cinnamon, salt, ginger, nutmeg, and cloves in a large bowl; set aside. Whisk together the pumpkin puree, oil, eggs, vanilla, and rice milk in a separate bowl until evenly blended. Add the pumpkin mixture to the dry ingredients and stir until fully blended. Pour into the prepared crust and place on a cookie sheet in the preheated oven.

Bake for 10 minutes. Reduce temperature to 350 degrees F (175 degrees C) and bake for 40 to 50 minutes or until a knife inserted near the center comes out clean. The center may still wiggle a little but will firm up out of the oven. Cool on a metal rack. SOUR CREAM APPLE PI

Servings: 8 | Prep: 30m | Cooks: 1h | Total: 1h30m

NUTRITION FACTS

Calories: 368 | Carbohydrates: 50.9g | Fat: 17.2g | Protein: 4g | Cholesterol: 44mg

INGREDIENTS

- 2 tablespoons all-purpose flour
- 3 cups apples, peeled and chopped
- 1/4 teaspoon salt
- 1 recipe pastry for a 9 inch single crust pie
- 3/4 cup white sugar
- 1/3 cup white sugar
- 1/4 teaspoon ground nutmeg
- 1/3 cup all-purpose flour
- 1 egg
- 1 teaspoon ground cinnamon
- 1 cup sour cream
- 2 tablespoons butter

1 teaspoon vanilla extract

DIRECTIONS

1. Stir together 2 tablespoons flour, salt, 3/4 cup sugar and nutmeg in bowl. Combine egg, sour cream and vanilla in another bowl; mix well. Add egg mixture to dry ingredients; mix well. Stir in apples and spoon mixture into unbaked pie shell.
2. Bake in a preheated 400 degree F (205 degrees C) oven 15 minutes.
3. Reduce temperature to 350 degrees F (175 degrees C) and bake 30 minutes more. Remove pie from oven. Increase temperature to 400 degree F (205 degrees C).
4. Prepare cinnamon topping and sprinkle over pie. Return to oven and bake 10 minutes more. Cool on rack.
5. To Make Cinnamon Topping: Combine 1/3 cup sugar, 1/3 cup flour and 1 teaspoon ground cinnamon in bowl. Cut in 2 tablespoons butter or regular margarine until crumbly, using a pastry blender.

BROWN SUGAR PIE

Servings: 8 | Prep: 30m | Cooks: 30m | Total: 1h

NUTRITION FACTS

Calories: 346 | Carbohydrates: 63.2g | Fat: 9.4g | Protein: 3.9g | Cholesterol: 29mg

INGREDIENTS

- 6 tablespoons all-purpose flour
- 4 tablespoons butter
- 2 cups packed brown sugar
- 1/2 teaspoon salt
- 1 1/2 cups evaporated milk

1 teaspoon vanilla extract **DIRECTIONS**

1. Preheat oven to 400 degrees F (200 degrees C).
2. In a saucepan, combine flour and sugar. Stir in milk, butter, salt and vanilla. Cook, stirring constantly, until mixture comes to a boil. Pour into an unbaked pie shell.
3. Bake at 400 degrees F (200 degrees C) for 5 minutes. Reduce heat to 350 degrees F (175 degrees C) and continue baking for 25 minutes.

BLUEBERRY 'S' PIE
Servings: 8 | Prep: 20m | Cooks: 45m | Total: 1h5m

NUTRITION FACTS

Calories: 469 | Carbohydrates: 60.8g | Fat: 24.3g | Protein: 4.2g | Cholesterol: 61mg

INGREDIENTS

- 1 cup butter
- 1 1/2 cups quick cooking oats
- 1 cup all-purpose flour
- 1/2 teaspoon salt
- 1 cup brown sugar

1 (15 ounce) can sweetened blueberries, drained**DIRECTIONS**

1. Preheat oven to 350 degrees F (175 degrees C).
2. In a medium bowl, cream together the butter and brown sugar. Stir in flour, salt and oats. Mix until well combined.
3. Pat 2/3 of the mixture into an ungreased 9-inch pie pan to form the bottom crust. Spread blueberries evenly into crust. Pat the remaining oat mixture onto top of blueberries.
4. Bake in preheated oven until topping is golden brown and filling is bubbly, 40 to 50 minutes.

STRAWBERRY PIE

Servings: 8 | Prep: 10m | Cooks: 10m | Total: 20m

NUTRITION FACTS

Calories: 537 | Carbohydrates: 96.8g | Fat: 16g | Protein: 4.9g | Cholesterol: 0mg

INGREDIENTS

- 2 1/2 cups water
- 1 (3 ounce) package strawberry flavored Jell-O mix
- 2 cups white sugar
- 2 quarts strawberries, hulled
- 5 tablespoons cornstarch

2 (9 inch) pie shells, baked **DIRECTIONS**

1. In a saucepan, combine water, sugar and cornstarch. Cook over medium high heat, stirring constantly, until mixture boils and thickens. Remove from heat and stir in the strawberry gelatin. Allow to cool slightly.
2. Arrange strawberries in the pie crusts with the tips pointing up. Pour gelatin mixture over, covering the berries.

SASKATOON PIE

Servings: 8 | Prep: 15m | Cooks: 1h | Total: 1h15m

NUTRITION FACTS

Calories: 366 | Carbohydrates: 52.3g | Fat: 16.6g | Protein: 3.6g | Cholesterol: 4mg

INGREDIENTS

- 4 cups fresh serviceberries
- 3 tablespoons all-purpose flour
- 1/4 cup water
- 1 recipe pastry for a 9 inch double crust pie
- 2 tablespoons lemon juice
- 1 tablespoon butter

3/4 cup white sugar**DIRECTIONS**

1. Preheat oven to 425 degrees F (220 degrees C).
2. In a large saucepan, simmer berries in 1/4 cup water for 10 minutes. Stir in lemon juice with berries. Combine sugar and flour together in a medium bowl, then stir into berry mixture. Pour mixture into a pastry lined 9 inch pie pan. Dot with butter. Place second crust on top of pie; seal and flute edges.

3. Bake in preheated oven for 15 minutes. Then reduce oven temperature to 350 degrees F (175 degrees C) and bake for an additional 35 to 45 minutes, or until golden brown.

CRANBERRY STREUSEL PIE

Servings: 8 | Prep: 30m | Cooks: 45m | Total: 1h20m | Additional: 5m

NUTRITION FACTS

Calories: 339 | Carbohydrates: 56.2g | Fat: 12.3g | Protein: 3.4g | Cholesterol: 0mg

INGREDIENTS

- 1 pound fresh cranberries
- 1/2 cup walnuts
- 3/4 cup white sugar
- 1/4 cup all-purpose flour
- 1/4 cup all-purpose flour
- 1 teaspoon shortening
- 1/2 cup packed brown sugar

1 recipe pastry for a 9 inch single crust pie **DIRECTIONS**

1. Preheat oven to 350 degrees F (175 degrees C).
2. Smash berries. Stir in sugar and 1/4 cup flour. Pour filling into pie crust.
3. Smash walnuts into small pieces. Stir in brown sugar, 1/4 cup flour, and shortening with a pastry blender. The mixture should be crumbly. Sprinkle streusel over pie.
4. Place pie on a baking sheet and bake in preheated oven until crust is golden and filling is bubbly, about 45 minutes.

GRAHAM CRACKER CRUST

Servings: 8 | Prep: 5m | Cooks: 1h | Total: 1h5m

NUTRITION FACTS

Calories: 175 | Carbohydrates: 20.4g | Fat: 10.2g | Protein: 1.2g | Cholesterol: 23mg**INGREDIENTS**

- 1 1/2 cups graham cracker crumbs
- 6 tablespoons butter, softened

1/3 cup white sugar

DIRECTIONS

1. Mix crumbs, butter, and sugar in a bowl. Press mixture into a 9-inch pie plate. Use a spoon to press the crumbs up the side of the plate and the side of your hand to press down on the top.
2. Refrigerate at least 1 hour before filling.

PEACH PIE WITH SOUR CREAM
Servings: 8 | Prep: 20m | Cooks: 1h15m | Total: 1h35m

NUTRITION FACTS

Calories: 337 | Carbohydrates: 45.2g | Fat: 16.1g | Protein: 3.8g | Cholesterol: 113mg

INGREDIENTS

- 1 1/4 cups all-purpose flour
- 3 egg yolks
- 1/2 cup butter, cut into chunks
- 2 tablespoons all-purpose flour
- 1/2 teaspoon salt
- 1/3 cup sour cream
- 2 tablespoons sour cream
- 1 cup white sugar

4 fresh peaches - peeled, pitted, and sliced

DIRECTIONS

1. Preheat oven to 425 degrees F (220 degrees C). Butter a 9-inch pie dish.
2. Place 1 1/4 cups flour, butter, salt, and 2 tablespoons sour cream in a food processor; pulse until mixture comes together in a large ball. Press dough into prepared pie dish to form a crust.
3. Bake in preheated hoven until golden brown, about 10 minutes. Remove pie crust from oven.
4. Reduce oven heat to 350 degrees F (175 degrees C). Arrange peach slices in pie crust.
5. Lightly beat egg yolks in a large bowl. Add in sugar, 1/3 cup sour cream, and 2 tablespoons flour; stir until well-mixed. Pour egg mixture over peaches. Cover pie with aluminum foil.
6. Bake in preheated oven for 50 minutes; remove foil. Continue baking until peach filling is set, about 15 minutes more.

EASY CHOCOLATE TOFU PIE
Servings: 8 | Prep: 15m | Cooks: 25m | Total: 40m

NUTRITION FACTS

Calories: 293 | Carbohydrates: 49.2g | Fat: 9.7g | Protein: 5g | Cholesterol: 0mg

INGREDIENTS

- 1 pound silken tofu
- 1 tablespoon vanilla extract
- 1/2 cup unsweetened cocoa powder
- 1/2 teaspoon cider vinegar
- 1 cup white sugar

1 (9 inch) prepared graham cracker crust **DIRECTIONS**

1. Preheat oven to 375 degrees F (190 degrees C).
2. Blend tofu with an electric mixer or in a food processor until smooth. Blend in cocoa, sugar, vanilla and vinegar. Pour into prepared crust.
3. Bake in preheated oven for 25 minutes.
4. Refrigerate for 1 hour before serving.

WALNUT PUMPKIN PIE
Servings: 8 | Prep: 10m | Cooks: 40m | Total: 50m

NUTRITION FACTS

Calories: 459 | Carbohydrates: 59.4g | Fat: 22.5g | Protein: 8.3g | Cholesterol: 48mg

INGREDIENTS

- 1 (9 inch) prepared graham cracker crust
- 1/2 teaspoon ground nutmeg
- 2 cups pumpkin puree
- 1/2 teaspoon salt
- 1 (14 ounce) can sweetened condensed milk
- 1/4 cup packed brown sugar
- 1 egg
- 2 tablespoons all-purpose flour
- 1 1/4 teaspoons ground cinnamon
- 2 tablespoons butter
- 1/2 teaspoon ground ginger
- 3/4 cup chopped walnuts

DIRECTIONS

1. Preheat oven to 425 degrees F (220 degrees C).
2. In a mixing bowl, combine the pumpkin, condensed milk, egg, 3/4 teaspoon cinnamon, ginger, nutmeg and salt. Pour batter into the pie crust.
3. Bake at 425 degrees F (220 degrees C) for 15 minutes. Reduce oven temperature to 350 degrees F (175 degrees C).

4. In a small bowl, combine brown sugar, flour, and remaining 1/2 teaspoon cinnamon. Cut in the butter or margarine until the mixture is crumbly. Stir in walnuts. Sprinkle mixture evenly over the pie. Bake pie for 40 minutes or until a knife inserted one inch from the edge comes out clean. Cool and garnish as desired.

ENGLISH WALNUT PIE

Servings: 8 | Prep: 20m | Cooks: 45m | Total: 1h5m

NUTRITION FACTS

Calories: 453 | Carbohydrates: 55.9g | Fat: 24.6g | Protein: 5.6g | Cholesterol: 85mg

INGREDIENTS

- 3 eggs
- 3/4 cup light corn syrup
- 1/4 teaspoon salt
- 1 cup chopped walnuts
- 3/4 cup white sugar
- 1/4 cup butter
- 2 teaspoons vanilla extract

1 (9 inch) deep dish pie crust **DIRECTIONS**

1. Preheat oven to 400 degrees F (205 degrees C).
2. Beat the eggs in a large bowl. Mix in sugar, salt, vanilla, and corn syrup. Melt the butter and whisk it into the egg mixture. Stir in the nuts. Pour filling into pie shell.
3. Bake in preheated oven for 10 minutes. Reduce heat to 300 degrees F (150 degrees C), and continue baking for 35 to 45 minutes.

STRAWBERRY PRETZEL PIE

Servings: 16 | Prep: 10m | Cooks: 2h30m | Total: 2h | Additional: 2h

NUTRITION FACTS

Calories: 332 | Carbohydrates: 43.6g | Fat: 17.3g | Protein: 3.4g | Cholesterol: 15mg

INGREDIENTS

- 2 cups coarsely crushed pretzels
- 1 (8 ounce) container frozen whipped topping, thawed
- 3/4 cup margarine, melted
- 2 (3 ounce) packages strawberry flavored Jell-O
- 1 tablespoon white sugar

- 2 cups boiling water
- 1 (8 ounce) package cream cheese, softened
- 2 (10 ounce) packages frozen sweetened strawberries (do not thaw)

1 cup white sugar

DIRECTIONS

1. Preheat oven to 400 degrees F (200 degrees C).
2. In a medium bowl mix together crushed pretzels, melted margarine, and 1 tablespoon sugar. Press mixture firmly into bottom of a 9x13 inch baking pan. Bake in preheated oven for 8 to 10 minutes, until lightly browned. Cool completely.
3. In a medium mixing bowl, beat together softened cream cheese and 1 cup sugar until smooth and fluffy. Fold in whipped topping and spread mixture evenly onto cooled crust.
4. Place gelatin in a medium heat-proof bowl and pour in boiling water. Stir gently until gelatin is completely dissolved. Add frozen strawberries and continue to stir until mixture begins to thicken. Chill until semi-firm but still pourable. Pour gelatin mixture over cream cheese layer. Chill at least 2 hours before serving.

BRIGID'S BLACKBERRY PIE

Servings: 8 | Prep: 15m | Cooks: 1h | Total: 1h15m

NUTRITION FACTS

Calories: 463 | Carbohydrates: 72.6g | Fat: 18g | Protein: 4.8g | Cholesterol: 4mg

INGREDIENTS

- 1 (15 ounce) package pastry for a 9 inch double crust pie
- 1/2 cup all-purpose flour
- 4 cups fresh blackberries
- 1/4 teaspoon salt
- 1 1/2 cups white sugar
- 1 tablespoon butter

DIRECTIONS

1. Preheat the oven to 325 degrees F (165 degrees C). Line a 9 inch deep dish pie pan with one of the crusts.
2. Place the blackberries in a large bowl. Stir together the sugar, flour, and salt. Sprinkle over the berries, and toss to coat. Pour into the pie crust. Dot with butter. Place the other pie crust over the top, and secure to the bottom crust by pressing with a fork, or fluting with your fingers. Cut a design in the top crust with a sharp knife to vent steam.
3. Bake for 1 hour in the preheated oven, or until the top crust is browned. Let cool to almost room temperature before serving to allow the filling to set.

CRUMB-TOPPED STRAWBERRY RHUBARB PIE

Servings: 8 | Prep: 30m | Cooks: 50m | Total: 1h20m

NUTRITION FACTS

Calories: 506 | Carbohydrates: 81.1g | Fat: 19.2g | Protein: 4.9g | Cholesterol: 41mg

INGREDIENTS

- 1 cup all-purpose flour
- 1/4 teaspoon ground nutmeg
- 1/8 teaspoon salt
- 2 cups rhubarb, sliced 1/2-inch thick
- 1/3 cup chilled butter
- 2 cups sliced fresh strawberries
- 2 tablespoons cold water, or more as needed
- 1/3 cup chopped pecans
- 1 1/4 cups white sugar
- 1 cup all-purpose flour
- 1/3 cup all-purpose flour
- 2/3 cup white sugar
- 1/2 teaspoon ground cinnamon

1/3 cup chilled butter **DIRECTIONS**

1. Preheat oven to 400 degrees F (200 degrees C). Whisk 1 cup of flour and salt in a bowl.
2. Cut 1/3 cup of butter into the flour mixture with a pastry cutter until the mixture resembles coarse crumbs. Moisten with water, 1 tablespoon at a time, just until the mixture holds together. Shape the dough into a ball, and roll out into a 12-inch circle on a floured work surface. Crust will be thin. Fold the dough gently into quarters, and lay into a 9-inch pie dish; unfold the dough and center the crust in the pie dish. Trim the crust to 1/2 inch of overhang, and crimp or flute the edge of the crust. Refrigerate crust while making filling.
3. Mix 1 1/4 cups of sugar, 1/3 cup of flour, cinnamon, and nutmeg in a bowl until thoroughly combined. Mix in the rhubarb and strawberries, and pour into the crust-lined pie dish. Sprinkle with pecans. Mix 1 cup of flour with 2/3 cup of sugar in a bowl, and cut 1/3 cup of butter into the mixture with a pastry cutter until the mixture resembles coarse crumbs; sprinkle the crumb topping evenly over the pie filling. Cover the edge of the pie with strips of aluminum foil.
4. Bake in the preheated oven until the crumb topping is golden brown and the filling bubbles around the edges, 50 to 60 minutes. Remove foil for the last 10 minutes of baking to brown the pie edge.

TOPLESS BLUEBERRY PIE

Servings: 8 | Prep: 30m | Cooks: 30m | Total: 1h

NUTRITION FACTS

Calories: 219 | Carbohydrates: 39.8g | Fat: 6.8g | Protein: 1.3g | Cholesterol: 4mg

INGREDIENTS

- 3/4 cup white sugar
- 4 cups fresh blueberries
- 3 tablespoons cornstarch
- 1 tablespoon butter
- 1 pinch salt
- 1 (9 inch) pie crust, baked

1 cup water

DIRECTIONS

1. In a saucepan, combine sugar, cornstarch and salt. Stir in water and 1 cup of blueberries. Cook and stir over medium heat, until thick, approximately 8 to 10 minutes.
2. Add butter and let cool about 5 minutes. Stir in remaining blueberries.
3. Pour into baked pie shell and cool in the refrigerator for 2 to 4 hours.

CHERRY PIE

Servings: 8 | Prep: 45m | Cooks: 40m | Total: 2h25m | Additional: 1h

NUTRITION FACTS

Calories: 348 | Carbohydrates: 47.4g | Fat: 16.6g | Protein: 3.6g | Cholesterol: 4mg

INGREDIENTS

- 1 pastry for a 9 inch double crust pie
- 3 tablespoons all-purpose flour
- 2 1/2 cups pitted sour cherries
- 1 tablespoon butter
- 3/4 cup white sugar

1 pinch salt **DIRECTIONS**

1. Preheat oven to 400 degrees F (200 degrees C). Line a 9-inch pie plate with pastry.
2. Mix the sugar, flour, and salt; toss with the cherries, mixing well. Pour the cherry filling into the pie shell, and dot with butter.
3. Weave strips of pastry into a lattice top. Place the pie on a baking sheet.
4. Bake in the preheated oven until the filling is bubbling and the crust is golden brown, about 40 minutes. Cool on a wire rack.

LEMON PIE

Servings: 8 | Prep: 5m | Cooks: 4h | Total: 4h5m | Additional: 4h

NUTRITION FACTS

Calories: 398 | Carbohydrates: 53.9g | Fat: 18.8g | Protein: 5.5g | Cholesterol: 17mg

INGREDIENTS

- 1 (14 ounce) can sweetened condensed milk
- 1 (8 ounce) container frozen whipped topping, thawed
- 1/2 cup lemon juice

1 (9 inch) prepared graham cracker crust **DIRECTIONS**

1. In a bowl, combine milk and lemon juice; mix until smooth (mixture will begin to thicken). Fold in whipped topping; spoon into crust. Chill until ready to serve, at least 4 hours or overnight.

YUMMY EGGNOG PIE

Servings: 8 | Prep: 30m | Cooks: 15m | Total: 4h45m | Additional: 4h

NUTRITION FACTS

Calories: 453 | Carbohydrates: 33.9g | Fat: 33.5g | Protein: 4.5g | Cholesterol: 110mg**INGREDIENTS**

- 1 (4.6 ounce) package non-instant vanilla pudding mix
- 2 cups heavy cream
- 1/4 teaspoon ground nutmeg
- 1 (9 inch) pie shell, baked
- 1 1/2 cups eggnog
- 1 pinch ground nutmeg

2 teaspoons rum

DIRECTIONS

1. In a medium saucepan, combine pudding mix, 1/4 teaspoon nutmeg, and eggnog; mix well. Cook over medium heat, stirring constantly, until thick and bubbly. Remove from heat, and stir in rum. Transfer mixture to a large bowl, cover, and refrigerate until thoroughly chilled.
2. In a medium bowl, whip the cream to soft peaks. Remove the cold pudding from the refrigerator, and beat until smooth; fold in whipped cream. Spoon into baked pie shell. Sprinkle additional nutmeg over the top for garnish. Refrigerate 4 hours, or until set.

MEXICAN PUMPKIN EMPANADAS
Servings: 12 | Prep: 40m | Cooks: 20m | Total: 1h

NUTRITION FACTS

Calories: 384 | Carbohydrates: 52.3g | Fat: 18.6g | Protein: 5.5g | Cholesterol: 47mg

INGREDIENTS

- 3 cups all-purpose flour
- 2 eggs
- 1/3 cup white sugar
- 1 cup white sugar
- 11/2 teaspoons salt
- 1 teaspoon salt
- 1/4 teaspoon baking powder
- 1 1/2 teaspoons ground cinnamon
- 1 cup vegetable shortening
- 1 teaspoon ground ginger
- 1 cup warm water
- 1/2 teaspoon ground cloves
- 4 cups canned pure pumpkin

1 beaten egg **DIRECTIONS**

1. Preheat oven to 350 degrees F (175 degrees C). Line baking sheets with parchment paper.
2. In a large bowl, whisk the flour, 1/3 cup of sugar, 1 1/2 teaspoons of salt, and baking powder together. Cut the shortening into the flour mixture until it resembles coarse crumbs; stir the water in, about 2 tablespoons at a time, just until you can gather the dough together. Knead the dough a few times in the bowl, then scrape it out onto a floured surface. Cut the dough in quarters, and cut each quarter into thirds to make 12 equal portions. Roll the portions into balls. Cover the dough balls with a cloth, and allow to rest while you make the filling.
3. Mix the pumpkin, 2 eggs, 1 cup of sugar, 1 teaspoon of salt, cinnamon, ginger, and cloves together until smooth. On a floured surface, roll each dough ball out into a thin circle about 6 inches across; spoon about 1/3 cup of filling into the center of the dough circle. Fold the dough over the filling to make a half-moon shaped pie, and crimp the edges of the crust together with a fork, leaving little fork lines in the dough. Gently lay the empanadas onto the prepared baking sheets. Brush the top of each pie with beaten egg.
4. Bake in the preheated oven until the filling is hot and the crusts are shiny and browned, about 20 minutes.

RUSTIC AUTUMN FRUIT TART
Servings: 8 | Prep: 15m | Cooks: 30m | Total: 1h45m | Additional: 1h

NUTRITION FACTS

Calories: 361 | Carbohydrates: 50.5g | Fat: 17g | Protein: 4g | Cholesterol: 46mg

INGREDIENTS

- 1/2 cup butter, chilled
- 1/3 cup brown sugar
- 1/2 cup cream cheese
- 1/2 teaspoon ground cinnamon
- 1 1/2 cups all-purpose flour
- 1/4 teaspoon ground nutmeg
- 2 apples - peeled, cored, and thinly sliced
- 1/4 teaspoon ground cardamom
- 1 pear - peeled, cored and sliced
- 1 1/2 tablespoons cornstarch
- 1/4 cup orange juice

1/2 cup apricot jam, warmed **DIRECTIONS**

1. Cut the cold butter and cream cheese into the flour with a knife or pastry blender until the mixture resembles coarse crumbs. (This can also be done in a food processor: pulse the cold butter into the flour until the mixture resembles cornmeal; add the cream cheese and pulse until it's the size of small peas.) When you squeeze a handful of the mixture, it should form a ball. Shape the dough into a round disk, wrap it in plastic, and refrigerate for at least 1 hour.
2. Toss the sliced apples and pear with the orange juice. Whisk together the brown sugar, cinnamon, nutmeg, cardamom, and cornstarch. Toss the fruit with the sugar-spice mixture and set aside.
3. Preheat an oven to 375 degrees F (190 degrees C). Set out an 8-inch tart pan, or, if you'll be making a free-form tart (galette), lightly grease a baking sheet.
4. Roll the pastry out on a lightly floured work surface to form a 10-inch circle. Transfer the dough to the tart pan or baking sheet. Arrange the fruit decoratively in the tart pastry. If you're baking the tart on a baking sheet, leave a 2-inch rim of dough and fold it up over the edge of the fruit (the pastry folds will overlap).
5. Bake the tart in the preheated oven until the crust is browned and the filling is bubbly, about 30 minutes. Remove the tart from the oven and brush it with the apricot jam.

MUM'S IRISH APPLE PIE
Servings: 8 | Prep: 1h15m | Cooks: 45m | Total: 2h

NUTRITION FACTS

Calories: 527 | Carbohydrates: 61g | Fat: 30.5g | Protein: 5.4g | Cholesterol: 87mg

INGREDIENTS

- 1 1/2 cups all-purpose flour
- 1/8 teaspoon lemon juice
- 3/4 cup cake flour
- 5 large Granny Smith apples - peeled, cored and sliced
- 1/2 teaspoon salt
- 1/2 cup white sugar
- 1 tablespoon white sugar
- 2 tablespoons all-purpose flour
- 1 cup unsalted butter
- 1/2 tablespoon ground nutmeg
- 3 tablespoons shortening
- 1/8 teaspoon lemon juice
- 1/4 cup sour cream

1 egg, beaten **DIRECTIONS**

1. Preheat oven to 350 degrees F (175 degrees C). Grease a 9 inch pie pan.
2. To Make Crust: In a large bowl, combine flours, salt and sugar. Cut in butter and shortening until coarse crumbs are formed. Mix in sour cream and lemon juice. Keep mixing until dough forms a ball; dough may be slightly lumpy, this is fine. Wrap dough ball in plastic wrap and allow to chill for 1 hour.
3. Once chilled, take dough out of refrigerator and cut it in half; keep one half covered and in the refrigerator. Roll dough to 1/8 of an inch. To lift pie shell, roll dough around rolling pin and then unroll into pie pan. Trim overhanging edges of pie crust.
4. To Make Filling: Place apples into pie shell. In a small bowl, combine sugar, flour and nutmeg; mix thoroughly. Sprinkle mixture over apples. Squirt lemon juice over apples. Place pie in refrigerator while top crust is rolled out.
5. Remove pie from refrigerator. Brush outer edge of bottom crust with beaten egg. Place second crust on top of pie; crimp pie shell edges together. Brush entire top crust with egg and cut 4 steam slots into it.
6. Bake in a preheated 350 degrees F (175 degrees C) oven for 45 minutes, or until golden brown. Allow pie to completely cool before serving. Serve warm with whipped cream or vanilla ice cream.

PINK LEMONADE PIE

Servings: 16 | Prep: 10m | Cooks: 2h | Total: 2h10m | Additional: 2h

NUTRITION FACTS

Calories: 253 | Carbohydrates: 36.9g | Fat: 11g | Protein: 3g | Cholesterol: 8mg

INGREDIENTS

- 1 (14 ounce) can sweetened condensed milk

- 1 (8 ounce) container frozen whipped topping, thawed
- 1 (6 ounce) can frozen pink lemonade concentrate, thawed

2 (8 inch) prepared graham cracker crusts **DIRECTIONS**

1. In a large bowl, mix together sweetened condensed milk and lemonade concentrate. Fold in whipped topping. Pour into pie crusts. Refrigerate until completely chilled.

CHEDDAR PEAR PIE
Servings: 6 | Prep: 20m | Cooks: 45m | Total: 1h5m

NUTRITION FACTS

Calories: 547 | Carbohydrates: 87.3g | Fat: 21.1g | Protein: 6g | Cholesterol: 30mg

INGREDIENTS

- 1/2 cup all-purpose flour
- 1 tablespoon fresh lemon juice
- 1/2 cup brown sugar
- 1/2 cup brown sugar
- 1/2 cup shredded Cheddar cheese
- 3 tablespoons cornstarch
- 1/4 cup butter
- 3/4 teaspoon ground cinnamon
- 6 cups peeled and sliced pears

unbaked pie crust **DIRECTIONS**

1. Preheat the oven to 400 degrees F (200 degrees C).
2. Combine the flour, 1/2 cup brown sugar, and Cheddar cheese. Cut in the butter until the mixture resembles coarse crumbs.
3. Toss the sliced pears with the lemon juice. Combine the 1/2 cup brown sugar, cornstarch, and cinnamon in a separate bowl. Add the sugar mixture to the pears and toss to coat.
4. Transfer the pears to the pie crust and top with the crumble mixture. Bake in the preheated oven until the top is golden brown, about 45 minutes.

SEX IN A PAN
Servings: 12 | Prep: 30m | Cooks: 1h | Total: 1h30m | Additional: 1h

NUTRITION FACTS

Calories: 463 | Carbohydrates: 44.5g | Fat: 30.6g | Protein: 5.9g | Cholesterol: 25mg

INGREDIENTS

- 1/2 cup margarine, melted
- 4 cups frozen whipped topping, thawed
- 1 cup chopped pecans
- 1 (3.9 ounce) package instant chocolate pudding mix
- 1 1/2 cups graham cracker crumbs
- 1 (3.4 ounce) package instant vanilla pudding mix
- 1 (8 ounce) package cream cheese
- 3 cups milk
- 1 cup confectioners' sugar

1 (1 ounce) square unsweetened chocolate, melted **DIRECTIONS**

1. Preheat oven to 350 degrees F (175 degrees C).
2. To Make Crust: In a medium bowl, mix together margarine, pecans and graham cracker crumbs. Pat into a 9x13 inch baking pan. Bake in preheated oven for 20 minutes or until lightly browned; allow to cool completely.
3. In a medium bowl, beat together cream cheese and confectioners sugar until smooth. Fold in 1 cup of the whipped topping. Spoon mixture into graham cracker crust.
4. Prepare chocolate and vanilla puddings with milk as per package directions. Allow pudding to set before pouring on top of the cream cheese layer. Spread remaining 3 cups of whipped topping over pudding layer; swirl melted chocolate throughout whipped topping.
5. Cover and refrigerate for about an hour. For leftover pie, keep frozen in a tightly covered container. When ready to eat, just cut off a piece and allow to thaw; keep rest frozen.

Printed in Great Britain
by Amazon